adam sandler

adam sandler

an unauthorized biography

D AVE S TERN

R ENAISSANCE B OOKS
Los Angeles

Library of Congress Cataloging-in-Publication Data [tk]
ISBN: 1-58063-121-5

10 9 8 7 6 5 4 3 2 1

Design by Susan Shankin

Published by Renaissance Books
Distributed by St. Martin's Press
Manufactured in the United States of America
First Edition

TO TEAM SANDLER
NICE WORK

acknowledgments

Thanks to Madeleine Morel, who encouraged me to do this project; the libraries (Neilson & Forbes) of Northampton, Massachusetts; the good folks (and the good coffee) at JavaNet; the people of Manchester, New Hampshire, who kindly showed me around their town; Sachdeep Arora, Michael Clemons, Bob Schiavone, Bill Thompson, and Pam Weinreich, who discussed Adam Sandler at length with me; and Allan Taylor whose keen eyes prevented more than one error from seeping through the text.

Thanks also to Jared and Seth at Seth Poppel's Yearbook Archives; Arlette Santos and Larry Schwartz at Archive Photos; Holly and Jenny at Wide World Photos; Jani Klain of the Museum of Television and Radio; Abigail Park and everyone else at Renaissance Books; and, of course, Jill, Madeleine, Toni, and Cleo, who had to suffer through my late-night laughing fits while I watched videotape after videotape featuring this book's subject.

Special thanks to Jim Parish, my editor on this book, whose patient guidance was key to this project's completion. I owe you one, Jim.

contents

introduction

"To know him is to love him."

ACTOR HENRY WINKLER

(Coach Klein in *The Waterboy*), discussing Adam Sandler, 1998

NO MATTER WHAT THE TIME OF YEAR, the walls of New York City's subway stations are plastered with movie posters. But as the days grow warmer, and the end of the school year approaches, those surfaces seem to become even more crowded than usual. The reason? Summer is blockbuster season—the most lucrative time of year for the major studios, those few months when they roll out their biggest guns, the movies that will to a large extent determine how their bottom line looks at the end of the fiscal year. Summer is blockbuster season because that's when teenagers (a group industry observers estimate is responsible for close to 40 percent of U.S. movie ticket sales) are out of school.

The studios target the vast majority of films released in these hot-weather months to capture that crowd.

Summer 1999's biggest gun was *Star Wars: Episode I—The Phantom Menace,* George Lucas's first Star Wars movie in twenty years. Walking through Manhattan's West Fourth Street subway station—the city's busiest, located in the heart of Greenwich Village—posters for that film, and its countless promotional partners (the Taco Bell Chihuahua, Colonel Sanders, the Pizza Hut delivery girl) seemed omnipresent. Yet right alongside that familiar *Star Wars* logo, standing out by virtue of its very simplicity was one for *Big Daddy.* In contrast to the usual movie ad posters, which contain bold illustrations of the stars and/or enticing scene shots, this advertisement for the new Adam Sandler movie was an all-type poster, black letters set against a light green background.

The *Big Daddy* poster consisted of just six words:

Adam Sandler
Big Daddy
June 25th

There could have been no surer sign that the former *Saturday Night Live* (1990–95) repertory player had ascended into the stratosphere of box-office attractions than this kind of promotional treatment, reserved for A-list stars like Tom Cruise, Harrison Ford, and Jim Carrey. Actors whose name is as close to a guarantee as one could get to a movie's box-office success.

Adam Sandler and Tom Cruise mentioned in the same breath?

Wait. It gets better.

People magazine recently released a list of the top five most requested celebrity photographs for their 25th Anniversary Photo Collection. Those five celebrities? Tom Cruise, Muhammad Ali, Madonna, Rosie O'Donnell, and . . . Adam Sandler.

Here's another surprising statistic: Adam Sandler's two 1998 films, New Line Cinema's *The Wedding Singer* and Touchstone's *The Waterboy,* together earned close to a quarter-billion dollars in U.S./Canada box-office receipts alone.

It's no wonder, then, that Sony Pictures felt confident enough to release *Big Daddy* on June 25, in the heart of the summer film season, where not only would it have to deal with the lingering effects of the *Phantom Menace* juggernaut but the cream of the competition's crop: Disney's newest animated feature, *Tarzan,* Warner Bros.' remake of *The Wild, Wild West* (starring Will Smith), and New Line's *Austin Powers: The Spy Who Shagged Me.*

Sony could have picked a safer corridor for *Big Daddy* to open in: After all, despite Sandler's remarkably successful 1998, all his previous films—not just *The Waterboy* and *The Wedding Singer,* but also *Billy Madison* (1995), *Happy Gilmore* (1996), and *Bulletproof* (1996)—were non-peak season releases. The studio believed in their new star, however, and it wasn't shy about letting the world know it.

Several months before the film's release—back on March 10, 1999, in fact—Richard Fay, president of film marketing for the AMC theater chain, had told the *Hollywood Reporter:* "*Big Daddy* sits there on June 25. It shows you that Sony is confident in what they've got. . . . You know that Sony expects big bucks."

Those theater owners had shown their own confidence in Adam by bestowing on him an honor unique in motion picture history: Sandler is the only person to have won both the ShowEast and the ShoWest Comedy Star of the Year award. With *Big Daddy,* they were clearly expecting him to return the favor.

He did so . . . in spades.

As of this writing, *Big Daddy* has grossed over $163 million, surpassing the $120 million total *Premiere* magazine, in its preview of 1999 summer blockbusters, had predicted for the film. Once again, the motion picture industry had underestimated the size of Adam's audience—and his uncanny ability to deliver what that audience wanted.

The size of that fan base first caught the entertainment industry by surprise in 1998, when they helped *The Waterboy* open with a record-breaking $39 million box-office weekend.

"We picked our stars, and these kids are picking their own," said the former chairman of Universal Pictures, Casey Silver, to Matthew Brelis of the *Denver Post* (April 13, 1999). And Sandler's one of the biggest: He's already received three MTV movie awards, including one at the 1999 Awards Ceremony for his work in *The Waterboy*. He's this year's Oscar Jr. winner for Male Role Model, a Nickelodeon Award Winner for Favorite Movie Actor (where his *The Wedding Singer* costar, Drew Barrymore, took home the trophy for Favorite Movie Actress), and winner of the Blockbuster Entertainment Award for Best Comedic Performance for *The Waterboy*.

In addition, he's also put out three best-selling comedy albums, two of which have gone platinum (sales of one million units) and were nominated for Grammy Awards. (A fourth album was released in the fall of 1999.) Turn on the radio during the holiday season, and you're likely to hear his "Chanukah Song," which, since its release in 1996, has become a seasonal favorite.

Sandler's ability to deliver what his audience wants in each of his films makes him unique among his comedic contemporaries. Although others may have hit bigger home runs (Mike Myers with 1999's *Austin Powers: The Spy Who Shagged Me* or Eddie Murphy with the first *Beverly Hills Cop* in 1984), they've also had their share of flops (i.e., Myers's *So I Married an Axe Murderer* in 1993 or Murphy's *Boomerang* in 1992). To date, each of Adam's succeeding films has outgrossed the previous one.

Although other comic talents are equally sure who their target audience is—David Spade clearly had teenage males in mind when he made *Lost & Found* (1999), as did the late Chris Farley when he starred in *Beverly Hills Ninja* (1997)—Adam is the only comedian of his generation who's been able to capture that audience with *each* of his films.

It's not just luck. Sandler's been very much in control of his destiny every step of the way. As Robert Simonds, who's produced all of Sandler's movies, told the *New York Times:* "Usually in the movies you're servicing a director's vision. [But] an Adam Sandler movie is all Adam Sandler. The sensibility and point of view is consistent and idiosyncratic."

Some critics have slammed that consistency, equating it with predictability. As Kendall Hamilton wrote in the November 11, 1998, issue of *Newsweek* magazine: "There's a formula to [Sandler's movies]. . . . Underdog rises to the top, falls, is redeemed, has a minor setback, rises again, and scores." But just because something is formulaic doesn't mean it's bad. Some of the biggest movie stars in history—from John Wayne and Cary Grant to Sylvester Stallone and Julia Roberts—have depended on formula. Or perhaps, their audiences demanded formula in order to see their idols fulfilling their expectations in a familiar way.

Adam Sandler as Happy Gilmore and Adam Sandler as the Waterboy clearly have a lot in common. Those characters share a persona, in fact, with their creator: a persona that, although occasionally crude, is never threatening, obnoxious, or mean. (When asked in 1999 by *E! Online* why he favored playing guys "who are just on the edge of being pathetic," Adam responded, "I like people in those situations. I'm not comfortable being around too many people. I don't like being out in public too much. I don't like going to bars. I don't like doing celebrity stuff. So most of the characters I play are people who don't always feel comfortable beyond their small circle of friends.")

"If you think of why Adam's got this following," Dennis Dugan—who directed Adam in both *Happy Gilmore* and *Big Daddy*—told writer Steven Schaefer of the *Boston Herald,* ". . . the central thing from 'SNL' on is: He's a really decent human being."

"He plays guys you want to root for, even if they're really screwed up. You want the guy to get it together, to figure it out," actor Steve Buscemi told *People* magazine in November 1998.

Buscemi's "you" includes millions of Americans—but not, however, a great many of the country's film critics. In fact, it would be fair to say that at this point in time, no star of Adam's caliber is as routinely belittled in the press as he is.

Adam seems to take the brunt of the criticism for what the media perceives as the dumbing-down of American movies, as represented by such recent pictures as *There's Something About Mary* (1998), *American Pie* (1999), and, of course, Adam's own films. One of Sandler's most savage critics, Richard Corliss of *Time* magazine, recently dubbed Adam "the Dominator of Dumb."

Given the lofty scale of Adam's recent success, however, even the mainstream press has been forced to take real notice.

Entertainment Weekly put him at number four on their 1998 Entertainer of the Year list. *People* magazine voted him one of the twenty-five most interesting people of 1998. And *Premiere,* in 1999, added him to their list of the 100 Most Powerful People in Hollywood (he came in at #56, sandwiched between Michael Douglas and Meg Ryan).

Not that Sandler cares much about any of his clippings—pro or con.

"I really don't pay attention to what the world says about my movies. I just care about what my buddies think," Adam recently told the Internet newsmagazine *E! Online.*

His buddies are the group of close friends who he's known since his days as a drama student at New York University, friends who, since his film career began, have helped him to make his movies the way he wanted. Buddies such as director Frank Coraci, actor Allen Covert, producer Jack Giarraputo, and writer Timothy P. (known to everyone as Tim) Herlihy.

This group of friends—stretch it to include producer Robert Simonds as well as director Dennis Dugan—has recently become known as "Team Sandler." They're Adam's support group: They help shield the very reticent celebrity from the probings of the outside world. (Occasionally, this same circle of pals lets the public in on at least some of what Adam is thinking—which, these days, is the only way to glean any real insight into what's on America's most press-shy actor's mind, because Adam himself stopped speaking to the print media in early 1998.)

It's nothing sinister, says director Dugan of Sandler's non-communication these days to the press. Regarding this unusual stance for a star, Dugan told reporter Louis Hobson of the *Calgary* (Alberta, Canada) *Sun*: "Adam is not a malicious kind of guy."

The director emphasized, "I don't think it's in his nature to take revenge [on the press who have frequently been severely critical of Sandler's movies]."

Dugan's statement about the origins of Sandler's avoidance of the press has the ring of truth. You'd be hard-pressed to find a more normal guy in the world of show business than Adam Sandler—an upbeat individual whose constant references over the years to his friends and family speaks volumes about his close and healthy relationships with both. Then too, despite the sometimes raunchy jokes that overlay Adam's movies, at their core, his pictures possess the same values as their creator: loyalty, heart, and (it almost goes without saying) an impeccable sense of comic timing.

Those same positive ingredients have served as the starting point for many a classic Hollywood comedy. They're qualities that Adam Sandler, at the ripe old age of thirty-three, appears to have mastered both on and off camera.

All of these factors should ensure that Adam—and Team Sandler—will be making movies for a long, long time to come.

CHAPTER 1

the outsider

"I think a lot of my comedy comes from the fact that

I'm Jewish, and I lived in a town full of no Jews. . . .

It made me develop some funny skills."

ADAM SANDLER, 1995

H E USED TO PRACTICE HIS COMEDY routines in the bathtub.

It's entirely possible, in fact, that the "shampoo vs. conditioner" scene in Adam Sandler's first starring vehicle, the film *Billy Madison* (1995), was a bit that he'd been rehearsing ever since he was old enough to speak.

The Adam Sandler story begins—like that of so many other great comedians (Woody Allen, Jackie Gleason, and Eddie Murphy, to name but a few)—in Brooklyn, New York. Adam was born there, on September 6, 1966, the youngest of Stan and Judy Sandler's four children—after brother Scott, and sisters Valerie and Elizabeth.

Pictures of the young Adam show a smiling child, with prominent front teeth and a headful of big, thick curly hair (this was the 1970s, after all). Details of his earliest years are sketchy: His family lived in an apartment in Brooklyn Heights, a residential neighborhood—historically, the city's first real suburb—just over the Brooklyn Bridge from Manhattan. Adam's father, Stan, was an electrical engineer; his mother, Judy, a homemaker; and his siblings were all good students, even in grade school.

Adam's first comedic impression was his dad's very individualistic sneeze.

"He goes 'Ayeestra!'" Adam informed reporter Janet Weeks of *USA Today* in February 1998. "It sounds like a Hebrew word."

The impression made his mother laugh—something that Adam would be doing a lot in years to come.

Brooklyn has provided the world with a wealth of comic stereotypes—from the mobsters of Bay Ridge to the homeboys of Flatbush, from television's Ed Norton (of the 1950s sitcom series *The Honeymooners*) to Spike Lee's Mars Redmond (from Lee's debut feature film, 1986's *She's Gotta Have It*). For many years, though, the most visible face of Brooklyn's rich comedic legacy was a Jewish one.

That's because for many years Brooklyn's Jewish population was one of the largest in the world (taken as a whole, New York City's still is). That culture's comedic legacy—part fast-talking, wisecracking, street-smart cynic, part downtrodden, forever misunderstood, lovelorn sad sack—was Adam Sandler's birthright.

It's a legacy that was epitomized by the stand-up comedy of Jackie Mason and Alan King, by the big-screen antics of Jerry Lewis and the Marx Brothers, and the records of raucous Rodney

"I Don't Get No Respect" Dangerfield—all of which Adam's dad shared with his youngest offspring time and time again.

However, most of that father-son sharing happened in a very different kind of neighborhood, in a culture as far removed from that of Brooklyn Heights as one could get in America without traveling south of the Mason-Dixon line.

Act One of the Adam Sandler story starts in Brooklyn.

But the most important part of it takes place some two hundred miles to the north.

Forget the smiling face of TV's beloved sewer worker Ed Norton.

Think instead of the scowling visage of nineteenth-century statesman/politician Daniel Webster, one of the great orators in American history. Picture the somber face of venerated poet Robert Frost, or the unsmiling countenance of our fourteenth president, Franklin Pierce, whose sad duty it was to preside over an America in the 1850s on the verge of civil war.

Consider the image conjured up by a people whose motto is "Live Free or Die."

We're talking about New Hampshire, the so-called "Granite State." Hardly seems like the sort of place you'd expect to provide a fertile breeding ground in the later twentieth century for comedic talent. All the more surprising, then, that this is where Adam Sandler developed and nurtured the comedic persona that would ultimately make him a world-famous TV and movie star.

The family's move out of New York had been precipitated by a job offer Stanley Sandler received in 1972. Though electrical engineering is not a profession typically associated with New

Hampshire (people often confuse it with its more rural neighbor Vermont where, up until the 1970s, cows outnumbered people), the New England state is actually one of the more industrialized ones in the country. The Sandlers' new hometown of Manchester was then (as it is now) the state's largest city, its cultural and artistic capital and—like its namesake Manchester in England—a major manufacturing center.

Located twenty miles north of the New Hampshire/Massachusetts border, Manchester was incorporated in 1846. With a land area of 33.9 square miles, the city of just fewer than 100,000 in population straddles the Merrimack River, whose banks are lined by red-brick factory buildings that once housed textile mills and cigar manufacturers, and have since been refurbished to provide space for more high-tech industrial concerns (Velcro USA, Electropac, and Rockwell Automation, for example). Downtown Manchester—which includes the police station, city hall, and the Chamber of Commerce—is on the eastern bank of the river, as is the Currier Gallery of Art and the New Hampshire Center for the Performing Arts.

Relocating out of Brooklyn immediately offered a number of advantages to Adam's family. No sales tax, no income tax, a strong school system, low crime rate, low cost of living, and easy access to the great outdoors.

Still, for all its pluses and relative cosmopolitan air, to a Jewish family from Brooklyn, used to living in the middle of the excitement, sounds, and sights generated by six million people, the move must have generated major culture shock.

No one felt that shock more keenly than five-year-old Adam.

Elm Street is downtown Manchester's main thoroughfare: running parallel to the picturesque Merrimack River. It is lined by a score of commercial buildings, as well as a handful of honest-to-goodness skyscrapers. At the north end of town, though, the commercial structures disappear and the street widens, becoming a broad, tree-lined avenue. Behind low stone walls and steel gates, magnificent colonial and Victorian homes, as grand as any in New England, flank either side of the road.

As you drive north on Elm Street, heading toward Hooksett (Manchester's neighboring town to the north), you pass #2519 on the right. It is a four-story brick building that, on first glance, seems to fit in seamlessly with the pristine, ordered world on display along the avenue. Imposing facade, manicured lawn, everything just so.

But when you circle around the back and see the concrete playground that runs the length of the block, the basketball nets and the jungle gyms, the monkey bars and the parking lot, you realize that Webster Elementary (named after—who else?—the state's favorite son Daniel) has far more in common with the average American grade school than its upper-crust neighbors.

The neighborhood behind the school is almost prototypically suburban: a warren of crowded streets, where the houses are squeezed closer together, the lawns smaller, the styles more modest than those imposing residences along the main avenue. The Sandlers' new home was back among these streets. As the summer of 1972 was ending, they all were settling into their fresh surroundings, Valerie and Elizabeth in one bedroom, Adam and older brother, Scott, in another.

The children were also preparing to make an even bigger adjustment: heading off to their new classrooms in the fall.

They'd have to cope with unfamiliar teachers, making new friends, finding out what clothes were cool to wear and what music it was all right to listen to. Brooklyn slang was out: New Hampshire–speak ("wicked good") was in. The acclimation was certainly a much bigger deal for Valerie, Elizabeth, and Scott—more mature and more set in their ways and expectations—than it was for their younger brother.

Nonetheless, getting used to a new way of life was something that young Adam was not looking forward to.

Adam had initially tried to put a brave face on the move: His dad helped by telling him that New Hampshire had toy stores that sold an assortment of the boy's beloved G.I. Joe miniature play soldiers—just like Brooklyn. The youngest Sandler gave the New England state a big vote of confidence on hearing that good news about his soon-to-be new hometown.

He was not so sure, however, about Webster Elementary School, where he was enrolled.

At recess every day, while the other children ran outside to play dodgeball, Adam would quietly gather up his things, exit through the gate at the rear of the fenced-in playground, and walk back up the hill to his house. Of course his teacher—Mrs. Kendall—noticed Adam's early exit, but attributed it to a simple misunderstanding. Adam had no doubt assumed first grade, like kindergarten, was only a half-day. When the young Sandler boy returned after lunch, clutching his mother's hand, Mrs. Kendall thought the problem had been solved.

Except the same thing happened the next day . . . and the next, and the next.

Mrs. Kendall soon realized that Adam knew he was expected to be at school for the full day. He just needed to go home to see his understanding mom. Once there, he'd sit down at the kitchen table and talk to her while she made him his usual peanut butter and jelly sandwich. After he ate it, she'd walk him back to class.

This routine went on for the first few days, until Adam finally felt more comfortable in his new surroundings. Another problem soon arose at school, however, one that didn't disappear quite so quickly.

As an industrial city, Manchester had seen several waves of immigrants come to town to work in the factories and mills along the Merrimack. Canadians, Irish, and Germans, to name a few, established their own neighborhoods and organizations within the city, making their presence felt in social and political circles alike.

One group of transplants who never got around to establishing a substantial presence in Manchester, however, were the Jews.

It wasn't that the city was anti-Semitic and had deliberately chased them away: There was a Hebrew School to send the children to, and a temple (now, today, two) to worship at on Friday nights. There just weren't a lot of Jewish people in Manchester.

There were even fewer at Webster Elementary. Just two, in fact, in Adam's entire class . . . and he was one of them.

Young children, being quick to seize on what's different and make fun of it, wasted no time in making Adam their new target.

"Everywhere I went, I heard comments about being Jewish. And it would hurt," Adam told Meredith Berkman from *Mademoiselle* magazine in March of 1995. His father advised him to stand up for himself, which he did, getting into fights on more than one occasion because of those unpleasant remarks. He couldn't, however, defend himself physically against all his classmates. So he tried another tack.

He started making them laugh.

Surprise: The funnier he was, the more kids liked him. Humor is, after all, a classic psychological defense, a way of fitting in with your peers where you might otherwise stand out unfavorably. Humor is also a way to become the positive center of attention— which Adam soon discovered he didn't mind at all.

One of his earliest laugh-provoking bits was popping out his ever-present dental retainer. Later, when he was old enough to go to the movies alone with his pals, he developed another routine: providing running commentary for the benefit of the audience.

"The funniest stuff I did when I was little, first to sixth grade, was at movie theaters, screaming at the screen," Adam told writer Chris Willman of the *Chicago Tribune* in October of 1994. "The whole theater [would] laugh."

The adolescent was also beginning to develop his own sense of humor, discovering those performers, films, and television shows that he found especially funny. He wasn't making those discoveries all on his own, though. Adam had instructors on hand at home to assist him: his father Stan, and, to an even greater degree, his brother. Scott's affection for one film in particular would be a powerful influence on the shape of Adam's comedy for years to come.

○   ○   ○

Ask most people what they know about the Catskills Mountains area in central New York state, and chances are the first thing they'll bring up will be the movie *Dirty Dancing* (1986). This romantic musical, which starred Jennifer Grey as Frances "Baby" Houseman, a young Jewish girl on summer vacation with her family, and Patrick Swayze as Johnny Castle, her Gentile dance instructor, does a fairly accurate job of presenting life in the so-called "Borscht Belt" during its last big hurrah in the early 1960s. At that time it was the favored resort destination for thousands of Jews anxious to escape the sweltering summers of New York City.

This Borscht Belt—the Catskills—lies about a hundred miles northwest of the city, in Sullivan and Ulster Counties. The bigger hotels—the Concord, Grossinger's, Kutsher's—hosted grade-A talent like comedians Jackie Mason, Billy Crystal, Myron Cohen, and Milton Berle; musicians like Sammy Davis Jr. and Neil Sedaka; variety acts like dancer Gregory Hines; and family entertainers, Steve and Eydie Gorme, Donald O'Connor, and so forth.

During a vacation trip Adam Sandler made to the Catskills with his family in the early 1970s when he was around five or six years old, the youngster received his first exposure to the intriguing, exciting world of stand-up comedy where an experienced jokester could hold the audience within his grasp, manipulating their collective mood with his power to entertain. It was a memorable experience, one he recalled years later, but not because of the jokes, or the nightclub ambience, or anything at all, in fact, to do with comedy.

"The guy was missing a finger," Adam remembered in a 1996 interview with writer Karen Hershenson of the *Knight-Ridder/Tribune News Service*. "My dad was laughing his butt off. My brother loved the guy [too]." The youngest Sandler didn't quite know how to react. "I was just staring." Subconsciously, however, it was undoubtedly a strong lesson for the young boy, seeing firsthand the power a professional comic could have on his audience. It made a far stronger impression on Adam than even he realized at the time.

Far easier for Adam—after having failed to really appreciate the Catskills stand-up comic—was sitting down at home and listening to his father's favorite comedy albums, including ones by boisterous Rodney Dangerfield and satirical Mel Brooks (in particular, *The 2000-Year-Old Man*). "I loved anything that made my pops laugh," Adam revealed in a February 1999 interview with *Playboy* magazine," . . . [and] I couldn't believe how hard my dad laughed at the *2000-Year-Old Man* album." To keep the laughs coming, Adam also learned to memorize Rodney Dangerfield's lines and walked around the house doing that comedian's better known shticks for his father.

Stan Sandler also introduced his younger son to the classic comedians of his own youth: the Marx Brothers, Laurel & Hardy, and Jerry Lewis. These comics, and the movies they respectively starred in—*A Night at the Opera* (1935), *Way Out West* (1937), *Cinderfella* (1960), and so on—provided Adam's introduction to the fascinating world of cinema. (Adam recalls his dad waking him up one night around 1 A.M. because a Marx Brothers movie was coming on. Adam was five at the time.)

While Stan was showing Adam great performances by other comedians, his mother Judy was encouraging her younger boy to do a little performing of his own. When he was all of seven years old, she took him on a visit to a nearby nursing home. There she had him sing the impassioned ballad "Maria" from *West Side Story* to a group of residents. At home, she urged him to sing for the refrigerator repairman or whoever else happened to drop by the house. A few years later, she made him sing at his sister's wedding. "I was eleven," Adam would later tell *People* magazine, in March of 1998: "My mother threw me up there. I sang 'You're Sixteen,' the Ringo Starr song. It was the only song I knew all the words to."

Looking back to Adam's childhood, his parents—especially his doting mother—were early on convinced that their youngest child had a penchant for the world of entertainment. In a February 1995 interview with *Entertainment Weekly*'s Kate Meyers, Judy Sandler would recall, "He's always been funny; he always woke up in a good mood. We knew he would be an entertainer."

Even more so than his parents, however, it was Adam's four-year-older brother, Scott, who influenced and initially shaped his taste in comedy. At first indirectly, when Adam, to impress his big brother, memorized lines from Scott's favorite films, like 1974's *Young Frankenstein,* and later explicitly, by bringing home records by drug-culture comedians like Cheech and Chong for Adam to listen to.

It was Scott's taste in films that Adam followed too. Soon after the Sandler boys saw the movie *Caddyshack* (1980), Adam was memorizing lines from that comedy to quote for Scott and his pals.

By his own estimate, Adam has now seen *Caddyshack* more than three hundred times. In every interview he does, he repeatedly cites this Harold Ramis–directed screen fare as the single biggest influence on his comedy.

The 99-minute feature follows the goings-on at an ethnically restricted, plush golf course; specifically, the efforts of a millionaire to purchase the land the course is on and develop it. The R-rated movie, which proved to be a big box-office bonanza, starred Chevy Chase, Bill Murray, and in his first major film role, Stanley Sandler's preferred funnyman—Rodney Dangerfield.

Adam would point to Dangerfield as his own favorite comedian in a dialog with fellow comedian/actor and friend Ben Stiller for the December 1994 issue of *Interview* magazine. (During their joint conversation with *Interview*, Adam was very impressed that Ben—the same age as Adam and the son of comedians/actors Jerry Stiller and Anne Meara—had pictures of himself as an infant with Dangerfield.) Certainly it's worth noting the common threads between Dangerfield's first two major movies (*Caddyshack*, a 1980's golfing comedy, and 1986's *Back to School*, where the rotund, big-eyed comedian stars as a millionaire who goes to college to win a bet with his son) and Sandler's early starring features (1995's *Billy Madison*, where the title character goes back to finish high school to win a bet with his father, and 1996's *Happy Gilmore*, a golfing comedy).

Yet, although the subject matter may be similar, there's little of Dangerfield's comic persona to be found in Adam's. In fact, it's Bill Murray—who, as the demented assistant groundskeeper Carl in *Caddyshack*, seems to have been the biggest inspiration for many of the less-than-intellectually gifted characters played later by Adam in his screen vehicles.

Those feature films, of course, were still far in the future in the fall of 1978, as Adam prepared to enter Hillside Junior High School on Reservoir Avenue in Manchester, New Hampshire. Unfortunately, Adam's affection for dumb was about to carry over into real life.

○   ○   ○

"Dating Adam was like dating all Three Stooges at once," revealed Karen Churas in the *Globe* (July 27, 1999). Although Churas may not have been Sandler's first case of "puppy love," she certainly caused young Adam a fair share of heartbreak when the two of them split up.

"Adam tried to be brave about it," Karen informed the *Globe*. When she delivered the bad news, however, Adam "ran off laughing, crying, flapping his arms like a bird and hollering, 'She loves me! She loves me not!'"

Why did the two of them go their separate ways? "Adam got it through his head that the way to my heart was through humor . . . [but] I hated it," Karen Churas said.

Playing the funny man wasn't just getting in the way of young Adam's nascent love life. It was starting to affect his school grades.

By Adam's own admission, as well as in the eyes of his teachers, he'd always been an underachiever at school. In his 1995 interview with *Mademoiselle* magazine's Meredith Berkman, he confessed that sometime around the sixth grade, he simply stopped trying in school. "All of a sudden I said, 'What the hell. I can't take it anymore. I can't read and be so serious in class anymore.' I don't know why, but I just started goofing off."

His lack of academic ambition was evident to everyone, particularly when contrasted with his more studious elder siblings. Adam's parents were rightly worried.

"One time, my mother was yelling 'Why don't you ever try?'" Adam related to writer Berkman. "I had a tape recorder in my hand. When she stopped shouting, I played it back at her. She laughed for a half an hour."

Nothing the Sandlers did, it seemed, could get their younger boy to concentrate on his studies.

CHAPTER 2

the class clown

"He was a good kid. But he was full of hell."

MICHAEL CLEMONS,

Adam's eleventh-grade American history teacher, 1999

HIGH SCHOOL IS ALL ABOUT BEING COOL.
It's about having the right hairstyle, wearing the proper clothes, being part of the accepted crowd. It's about driving the approved type of car, listening to the correct music, hanging out in the "in" places.

In the 1950s, it was about rock 'n' roll, leather jackets, motorcycles, pink shirts, black ties, white bucks, and sock hops.

In the 1960s, it was long hair, flower power, ecology, the Beach Boys, and the Beatles.

In the 1970s, it was bell-bottoms, Led Zeppelin, Cher, and the movie *Star Wars* (1977).

For a brief moment (before the explosion of hair bands in mid-decade), the 1980s seemed like they would be the 1950s all over again, with leather-jacketed punk rock groups like the Clash and the Stray Cats ruling the airwaves, and greasers like Arthur "The Fonz" Fonzarelli (from the 1974–84 TV series *Happy Days*) splashed all across the television screen.

In fact, the cool, motorcycle-riding Fonz, a self-professed expert on girls and cars, was a particular hero of Adam's—as was the very popular actor who played him, Henry Winkler, with whom Adam would later work in the 1998 screen comedy that catapulted Sandler to movie superstardom, *The Waterboy*.

But we're getting ahead of ourselves.

Suffice it to say, as Adam Sandler prepared to enter high school in the fall of 1981, he had the same concerns as millions of other students his age across the country: getting along, fitting in, and being liked by his peers.

Adam's way of making all three of those things happen was to keep on doing what he'd done in grammar school with such marked success. He made himself the deliberate center of attention. He told jokes, and he performed for his friends. Manchester Central High was just his new forum.

Central High School is located northeast of downtown Manchester. As you enter the James Building—one of three structures in the school complex—on your left is a glass display case, filled with trophies given to the school newspaper, *The Little Green*. "Best Paper—Scholastic Newspaper Association" reads the placard affixed to each award: The case also contains a photo of

NBC-TV News reporter Tom Brokaw, holding up a copy of the school publication.

There is no picture of Adam Sandler on display . . . at least not yet.

If you walk down the hall just a few doors to the office of Central High's Principal, Bob Schiavone, however, you can conjure up Sandler's presence easily enough. Schiavone was Sandler's guidance counselor, and he has many fond memories of the student he today calls "mischievous." (One suspects that, back in the early 1980s, Adam might have conjured up other one-word epithets from his school counselor.)

"He got into a lot of trouble," Schiavone admitted in a May 1999 phone interview with this book's author. Adam's behavior wasn't destructive—he didn't break windows, or deface school property—but was disruptive. "He was always fooling around, always joking," recalls Schiavone. Even, Schiavone remembers, while Adam was getting punished.

Central High in the early 1980s had a policy called "internal suspension." Students who acted out or broke school rules were prohibited from going to class, but still required to be in school. They had to spend the school day in detention hall, where they were permitted to do whatever they wished.

Scheduled for a day of "internal suspension," Adam decided to pass the lengthy hours by watching television. He brought in a pillow, a portable TV set, and made himself comfortable with his favorite daytime programs, such as the quiz show *Family Feud* and reruns of *The Love Boat*. (This was in the days before VCRs were widespread, or otherwise Adam might have thrown one of those playback machines into his backpack too and spent his detention time watching, instead, his beloved screen comedy,

1980's *Caddyshack*.) Not exactly what the policy-makers who devised "internal suspension" had in mind.

"We hadn't made any rules against those things," Schiavone acknowledges, "but we sure did after that."

Adam did do other things than tell jokes during his high school years. Schiavone remembers the future movie star playing junior varsity sports, basketball, baseball, even a little field and track. Sandler was also (briefly) a member of the student council—and for much of his time at Central High, part of the school's drama club, the Masquers.

"He always wanted to be a performer," recalled Schiavone. "Not necessarily a comedian, but to get into films or television. Almost exactly what he's doing now."

Sandler and the Masquers put on their shows in the school auditorium, located in the Practical Arts building. Outside in the central courtyard stands a large statue of President Abraham Lincoln. Erected in 1910, it shows a seated Lincoln, chin resting on his hand, deep in thought.

You don't even need to close your eyes to picture Adam sitting on the statue's platform (perhaps, even, on the statue itself), telling jokes to all his school pals. Without trying hard, you can even sense the disapproving stares of teachers looking down from their classrooms on the young Sandler—including, perhaps, Isabel Pellerin. Now the school's vice principal, her office is located in the Practical Arts building, next to the school store, which sells sodas, snacks, caps, and T-shirts—none of which (yet) bear the image of the school's most famous alumnus.

During Adam's high school years, Ms. Pellerin was Adam's "official disciplinarian," responsible for keeping her infamous charge in line. It was not an easy task.

"You've seen his movies?" she told *People* magazine in a November 1998 interview. "That's the way he was here." She recalled Adam as a constant disruption, always fooling around, never taking himself—or anything—very seriously.

Sandler's entire crowd in high school was much the same, as he would later describe to Betsy Pickle from the *Knoxville* (Tennessee) *News-Sentinel* in a 1994 interview.

"My friends were wisea**es and they had that New England wisea** charm, you know. Just drivin' down the street, anything anybody did—'Hey, pal, what's up?'—just yellin' at people."

You can see the troublemaker's glint in Adam's eyes in virtually all the pictures taken of him at this time. It's not the look of a bad kid: more the stare of someone who will push the limits as far as you let him.

Another notable thing about all the snapshots of Adam from his high school years: his dark hair. He wore it long—or more precisely, big. The Sandler 'do of the early 1980s was closer to a mini-Afro than anything else, like that worn by the character Epstein in the TV sitcom *Welcome Back, Kotter* (1975–79). Coupled with the thick eyeglasses he sometimes wore, the teenage Sandler often has the look of, well, a dork.

(It should be noted that the 1980s shag haircut Adam would later adopt for his breakthrough screen performance in 1998's *The Wedding Singer* was actually a wig.)

As a young man not blessed with classically handsome features or a chiseled physique, Adam didn't always have the easiest time with the opposite sex. Michael Clemons, who taught Adam's eleventh-grade American history class, recalled one particular young lady who was distinctly *not* captivated by the Sandler charm.

"There was a girl named Linda St. Martin in the class—a very pretty girl. Adam had a wicked crush on her—he would walk into the classroom, turn to Linda, and say 'So, Linda, when are you gonna go out with me?' And she'd say to him, 'When hell freezes over.' Everybody got a kick out of that."

Clemons is now Central High's vice principal, his office just a few doors down the hall from Bob Schiavone's. Like the principal, he remembers Sandler's years at Central with bemused fondness. There is genuine affection in his voice when he speaks of Adam.

"There were some teachers who didn't like him," Clemons detailed in a recent phone conversation with this author, "but I always thought he was a good kid."

And a quick wit even then.

"We were talking about President Andrew Jackson's 1829 inauguration, which was kind of a free-for-all," Clemons says, laughing. "They invited everyone in the country to it. There were kegs of beer inside the White House, and all kinds of food as well. But once they got the party started, they had a hard time getting the people out. So they took the kegs, and put them out on the White House lawn. The people followed . . . and then Jackson locked the doors behind them! After I told that story, Adam stood up in the middle of the class, and shouted, 'Kegs in the White House! Now that Andrew Jackson was my kind of president!'"

Clemons was apparently Sandler's kind of teacher. For the rest of the school year, Adam's unbridled humor, rather than disrupting the class, actually augmented it. "He had these little fractured pieces of history he was always bringing up," Clemons recalls, bits of history that made a sometimes tedious topic jump vividly to life.

For his part, Adam seems to view his high school years through the same glass as his disciplinarian Isabel Pellerin. In a November 1987 chat with reporter Nancy West of the *Manchester* (New Hampshire) *Union-Leader* (his local paper), Sandler remembered spending most of his high school days in the principal's office—a memory contradicted in the same article by Bill Burns, who was Central High's principal during Adam's time there. Burns recalled Sandler as "an ambitious young man, with a great sense of humor," and went on to say, "any rumors he generates about his misdeeds is pure exaggeration."

One misdeed from Adam's time at Central High that was definitely not an exaggeration was what happened on "Lettuce Liberation Day." The school's cafeteria was serving tacos that day and somehow a great deal of the meal's shredded lettuce made its way into Adam Sandler's Spanish class, where Adam set it free . . .

By tossing it out the window!

"Yeah, I was a wise guy," Adam laughed, recalling the incident in a February 1995 piece in *Women's World,* headlined "They Were the Kids Principals Love to Hate." "But I never hurt anyone," the future celebrity also pointed out to the publication.

Whether they regarded his antics as disruptive or amusing, there's one thing that all his instructors agree on: The person he is now is the same boy they taught in high school.

A clown. A performer. A natural wit.

And, as it turned out, a pretty fair singer.

The heyday of classic rock bands like Led Zepplin, Aerosmith, and the Eagles, groups who lived by the saying "If it's too loud, you're too old," occurred in the late 1970s. Bands like these ruled the airwaves, and their guitar players—Jimmy Page, Joe Perry, and Joe Walsh—inspired legions of young boys to tune up their six-strings, turn up their amps, and form bands.

Adam Sandler was one of those young boys.

A recent MTV cable television special showed a picture of Adam in high school—same big hair, same goofy eyeglasses—intently hunched over a red Gibson SG, a solid-body, double cut-away guitar model. This is the same kind played (most famously) by Angus Young of AC/DC, Tony Iommi of Black Sabbath, and, more occasionally, Pete Townsend of The Who. Adam had several musical groups in high school, bands with names such as Spectrum, Storm, and Final Warning: Clemons recalls Adam performing frequently at assemblies and school dances.

Adam was not just the guitar player in most of those student bands. He was the singer, too, a talent Sandler's mother Judy had continued to encourage throughout his youth.

"She'd always like to hear me sing, and so she sent me to take some lessons," Sandler told the *Asheville Citizen-Times* of North Carolina in 1995. Adam can still remember his first school performance: He did the classic rock 'n' roll song "House of the Rising Sun" in a seventh-grade talent show.

"My mother [was] driving me home afterward, and she said 'You kept cracking your voice,'" Adam recollected in the same interview.

As he grew older, Adam considered pursuing his music career seriously, but he had little idea of how to undertake that. He thought it was all about getting discovered, he explained to the Asheville,

North Carolina, newspaper in 1995. "I [figured] some guy comes over to my basement and hears my band and is like, 'Hey, you guys, you're gonna be big!' and just [offers] me a contract."

Needless to say, Adam quickly found out that was not the way things worked in the real world.

When graduation day rolled around in June 1984, seventeen-year-old Adam was simply unprepared to choose a direction for his life. He'd scooped cones at the local ice cream shop, the Puritan, and gotten fired. He'd been a busboy and dishwasher at the Back Room Restaurant (a Manchester landmark), and gotten fired. "I worked in a gas station, too," Adam later told writer Elias Stimac of *Drama-Logue,* "and I didn't do well there."

Though he'd done well enough in school and on his College Board Scholastic Aptitude tests to be accepted into New York University (NYU) for the upcoming fall semester, his main accomplishment at Central High School was being voted "Class Clown." In contrast to his siblings, he felt academically and professionally inadequate. His sister Valerie was a dentist; Elizabeth was on her way to being a successful businesswoman; and Scott was currently attending Boston University Law School.

Adam didn't know what he wanted to be.

"When I was in high school, I would say to my brother 'What do I wanna do?'" he relayed in a June 1999 interview with MTV's Chris Connelly. "'I don't like anything, I'm not good at anything, I got fired at scooping ice cream cones, I'm not the best at working hard . . .'"

Older brother Scott thought he had the answer. Adam, he decided, should seriously pursue his dreams of being a comic.

It's no exaggeration to say that this conversation radically changed Adam's life.

"If he hadn't said to do it," Adam acknowledged in a 1994 dialog with *Interview* magazine, "I wouldn't have thought it was a normal thing to do. I would have said, 'Mom and Dad are going to get mad at me.' But because [Scott] told me to do it, and I knew that my parents respected his brain, I was like, 'He said to do it, so it must be O.K.'"

It's possible, of course, that Adam would have become a comedian even without the urging of his supportive sibling. After all, once he got to NYU, he fell in with a group of friends who— it's fair to say—appreciated his talent as much, if not more so, than his brother.

Whether or not Scott was ultimately responsible for Adam's decision to become a comedian, Adam's older brother definitely deserves the credit for arranging Adam's first performance as a stand-up comic.

Comedy made a strong comeback in the early 1980s. Funnymen (and women) were suddenly fashionable again. Venues like the Improv and the Comedy Club opened to big business in cities nationwide. A rash of cable television shows put stand-up comedians in living rooms every night.

The hottest scene in the country at the time was in Boston, Massachusetts—just a little more than an hour southeast of Manchester. In Beantown, up-and-coming comics such as Jay Leno, Steven Wright, Paula Poundstone, and Barry Crimmins were drawing national attention for their performances. (It was also the city where future TV talk-show maven, Rosie O'Donnell, began her comedy career in the local clubs.)

Boston was also where Scott Sandler was attending Boston University Law School. One night, when Adam was visiting his brother, the Sandler duo decided to take in an evening of stand-up.

They went to Stitches, a comedy club over on Commonwealth Avenue. In those days, Stitches was comedian Kevin Meaney's home turf. Meaney's best-known routine (one he would repeat on an HBO cable TV special in 1994) was to leave the club, microphone in hand, video-cam-wielding assistant in tow, and pick on people: passing pedestrians, slow-driving motorists, whoever got in his reach. (Meaney was also known to walk out into the middle of busy Commonwealth Avenue and stop traffic in his search for improvisational material.) Whatever Meaney saw, whatever he said, was then broadcast back into the club.

The night Adam and Scott arrived, though, Meaney was not on hand. Instead, it was open mike night—the weekly ritual where any brave enough would-be comedian could get in front of the audience and tell jokes, stories, do impressions—whatever they thought (or hoped) was funny. At Stitches—as at any open-mike night—the quality of the performances tended to be wildly uneven, but that didn't affect Adam's reaction.

"I go to this place, and watch a night of comedy and holy cow I loved it," Sandler recalled in his mid-1999 conversation with MTV's Chris Connelly. "It was the first thing I remember thinking, not that I could be great at that, but I think I could get into that."

Get into it he did—that evening, in fact. Seemingly fearless, Adam jumped up onto the stage and gave an impromptu performance, relying again on the jokes that had once made his peers at Central High School back in Manchester, New Hampshire, laugh time and time again.

The response to Adam at Stitches, however, was not overwhelmingly positive.

"I tried the retainer thing," he would later tell writer Jennifer Weiner of the *Knight-Ridder/Tribune News Service* (February 1996), "and they were like, 'Look kid, just don't make us sick.'"

It was not an auspicious debut. And though Adam would spend the entire summer of 1984 performing as often as he could in the Boston nightclubs, none of his performances were particularly well received by local audiences.

"It [my comedy routine] didn't go right for a long time," Adam admitted to *Boston Herald* writer Dean Johnson in June 1996. "I didn't know what to do or what I was doing. I had no point of view."

Sandler's stage material reflected his life to that point—the life of an average American teenager. In his search to be funny, Adam talked to the audiences about girls; he made "humorous" observations about cars; he chatted "pointedly" about the Burger King fast-food chain restaurant back on Manchester's DW highway.

He talked too fast. The truth was, despite his bravado and surface ease, Adam was very nervous.

"I'd get very scared going out in front of a crowd. I'd have a gig on Tuesday, and I'd be a wreck for two weeks before. I'd panic and stutter and lose my breath out there," Adam later told the *Los Angeles Daily News'* Bob Strauss, in February 1998. Again, it was his highly supportive brother Scott who made a critical suggestion that helped Adam smooth out his performance routines.

"[He] suggested that I sing some songs, so I'd have words that I'd know I was going to say and not have to try to come up with things off the top of my head." Thus, Adam was urged to open his shows with a funny song or two to get comfortable on stage. The advice made perfect sense to Adam—who, after all, at that point had had far more experience in front of a crowd as a musician than as a comic.

"When you have a guitar in your hand, you don't have to be thinking as much. You're prepared, you have your three-minute song ready to go . . . [Scott's suggestion] definitely helped," Adam would later tell writer G. Brown of the *Denver* (Colorado) *Post* in a 1996 interview.

Just as Sandler was starting to get comfortable on the Boston comedy club stages, however, his summer of informal apprenticeship ended.

In the fall of 1984 Adam Sandler headed for the Big Apple—New York City.

CHAPTER 3

the big city

"The reason we were first friends is that I couldn't

believe some of the stuff coming out of his mouth.

It's the stuff we think but don't say."

TIM HERLIHY, PRODUCER OF NBC-TV'S

Saturday Night Live, 1999

COLLEGE IS ALL ABOUT MAKING CONNECTIONS.
The friends you make there are likely to be your best friends for life. Your first major romance will likely take place during your undergraduate years. It's more than likely that the career counseling you receive during college will determine your permanent choice of a profession.

For most, college helps you define who you are, and who you want to become. In many ways, college is even more cliquish than high school, but its tight-knit associations are based more on common interests than on mutual popularity. Pre-med students hang out together and talk about which prestigious medical schools they're going to apply to; business majors concurrently watch the stock market and talk about "emerging growth areas." If you're a history major, you'll congregate in the library stacks with your peers; if you're devoting yourself to the study of literature, you'll attend readings of Shakespeare's sonnets and form Chaucer appreciation societies.

If you're Adam Sandler, you'll meet the people with whom you'll spend the rest of your life making hit movies.

Thus, he met people such as Jack Giarraputo, who's produced (or helped produce) every one of Adam's starring films; Allen Covert, who's had roles in virtually all of Adam's showcasing features; Frank Coraci, who directed *The Wedding Singer* (1998) and *The Waterboy* (1998); and writer Tim Herlihy, who has co-written every one of Adam's headlining pictures, with the exception of Sandler's 1996 cinematic misstep, *Bulletproof*.

All four entered New York University (NYU) as members of the fall 1984 freshman class, as did Adam Sandler. They all lived in Brittany Hall, an NYU dorm located on East Tenth Street, just off Broadway in Greenwich Village. Herlihy was Sandler's roommate, while Giarraputo was Coraci's. (Covert and Sandler met later, in a class the two took together.) In the same dorm were future film editor Tom Lewis and scriptwriter Judd Apatow—who would end up marrying actress Leslie Mann, Adam's costar in *Big Daddy* (1999).

To call Brittany Hall a dorm may conjure up the wrong impression. The fifteen-story brick building is virtually indistinguishable from the many high-rise apartment houses surrounding it. You'd never know it was a college dorm were it not for the purple NYU flag flying in front.

NYU itself, despite its size (more than 5,000 students in each undergraduate class) also blends in seamlessly with (or perhaps, one should say, is swallowed up by) the Greenwich Village streets that form its campus. Those streets are mobbed virtually every night of the week by not just students, but the twentysomethings who drive Manhattan's night life. Hopping from club to club along Bleecker Street, seeking out the latest in music, comedy, theater, and films, they turn the area in and around Washington Square Park into a non-stop people-watching party that doesn't quiet down until the wee hours of the morning.

Adam and his new friends joined in that ongoing party enthusiastically. They put their stereo speakers in the dorm window and blasted Led Zeppelin tunes. They even put an amplifier in the same window and, using a microphone, insulted random passersby.

Of course, they all had their respective studies to attend to. Herlihy and Giarraputo were in business school, and Coraci was a film student.

And Adam was also hard at work, having been admitted to one of NYU's most exclusive, prestigious undergraduate programs.

Unfortunately, as in high school, Adam would again prove himself to be not the world's greatest student.

The Stanislavsky school of acting—"method acting" as it is more commonly known—stresses the use of "creative inspiration" as a basis for performance, a way of using your own life experiences to enhance the reality of the role you are now playing.

If it sounds complicated, don't worry. You're not alone. In 1984, it sounded abstruse to Adam, too.

"We were all supposed to go onstage and dig out our emotions," he recalled to writer Kevin Cook in *Playboy* (February 1999). "At that time I couldn't even look another person in the eye. I'm thinking, *Once I dig out my emotions, where do they go?*"

Method acting was what they taught at the prestigious Lee Strasberg Theatre Institute (Strasberg having been the Method's foremost teacher in this country at the time). As one of only 300 students accepted into NYU's drama program, Adam had the privilege of supplementing his liberal arts education with courses at the revered acting Institute.

It was a privilege that he—to put it charitably—did not take full advantage of. He didn't pay attention in class; he didn't take things seriously. As a result, the powers-that-be at the Institute thought of Sandler as a singularly inattentive student and were convinced he would never make the cut as a performer.

"The teachers didn't think he was serious," Geoffrey Horne, one of Adam's instructors, relayed to writer Betty Cortina in a conversation published in *Entertainment Weekly* (June 18, 1999). "One of them wrote an evaluation about Adam never being successful in the business."

It's hard to find fault with that assessment, given Sandler's level of performance in school. What none of Adam's teachers at Strasberg were seeing, however, was his act outside the classroom, where the always-less-than-perfect student had finally found something he was willing, even driven, to work at: his comedy act.

In a November 17, 1998, interview with writer Edie Jakes of New York City's local paper, *The Resident,* one time dormmate Frank Coraci talked about seeing the early Sandler performances.

"Adam [started off doing] stand-up at the dorm's coffee shop," Coraci remembered. "Then he formed a sort of comedy troupe—Adam and the Foreskins." His friends at Brittany Hall were no doubt an appreciative audience—but their applause wasn't enough for Sandler.

The eighteen-year-old comedian wanted the approval of a larger crowd. He became a tireless worker, sometimes devoting six nights a week trying out his new material in the many comedy venues of Manhattan and Brooklyn.

"It was great, watching, seeing what worked, what didn't, particularly in Brooklyn. When something didn't work, the crowd let you know it. [Adam] would just take material and work it until it was perfect."

Though Sandler was the one facing the audience, it wasn't long into his career before he had help devising his onstage material. As he would later tell online entertainment source *Hollywood.com* (in a November 1998 session): "[Tim] Herlihy went away one weekend to see his family, and he brought me back a piece of paper with a bunch of jokes and stories on it. I said 'You wrote this stuff for me?' He said, 'Yeah, you said you wanted to do stand-up. I figured I'd help.' And it was funny—funnier than the stuff I was writing."

Typically, when Sandler's stand-up act was done for the night, he and his friends would take the money he'd earned—usually about $10—and go to the Cozy Soup and Burger on Broadway for a late-night snack, or the Holiday Cocktail Lounge for a drink ("$1.25 for top shelf stuff," Coraci told *The Resident*'s Jakes in 1998. "You couldn't beat it.").

Ten dollars a night would hardly cut it in the real world, of course, so Adam and his buddies took other work to help make ends meet during the college year. Frank Coraci worked at the Antique Boutique—a vintage clothing store on Broadway that was extremely popular during the 1980s (an experience that was no doubt extremely helpful to him while filming *The Wedding Singer* set in that time period). For his part, Sandler had a number of odd jobs: counting pills in a drugstore, working as a waiter and a dishwasher, and even singing in the subways ("I'd open up my guitar case and sing Beatles tunes . . . when I got to $20 or $25 I'd buy food and go write some comedy," he told *Playboy*'s Kevin Cook in February 1999).

It was also about this time that Adam began to develop some solid ideas about the direction in which he wanted his career to go. One notion in particular captivated him: He wanted to become a member of the NBC network's late-night television institution, *Saturday Night Live* (otherwise known by its acronym *SNL*, 1975–present).

Adam had been too young to watch *SNL* during its glory years (1975–80), during the era of the original Not Ready for Prime Time Players (Dan Aykroyd, Gilda Radner, John Belushi, Jane Curtin, Chevy Chase, et al.). However, by the time he was in high school in the early 1980s, the weekly TV show had become a favorite of his. "Eddie Murphy stuck in my head. . . . He got to do whatever he wanted," Sandler recalled in a 1992 conversation with *Inside Media*'s Ed Martin. "That's the kind of humor I want[ed] to do . . . "

One of Adam's NYU classmates was Lorenzo Quinn, the son of Academy Award–winning movie star Anthony Quinn. At the time, Lorenzo moved in what were for Sandler rarified circles: His father, an actor for close to half a century, a two-time Oscar winner (1952's *Viva Zapata*, 1956's *Lust for Life*), had access to everyone who was anyone in New York entertainment circles. It was the two Quinns, father and son, who introduced Adam to the man who would help him take his performing career to the next level.

○ ○ ○

In 1987, the unquestioned King of Comedy was veteran entertainer Bill Cosby, who had begun his career decades ago in the world of stand-up comedy. Now as star and executive producer of NBC's *The Cosby Show* (1984–92), shot in NBC's New York facilities, Cosby had virtually transformed the landscape of television comedy. With its depiction of an upper-middle-class, African-American family in Brooklyn, it proved to critics that network television could produce programming of genuine human interest. It also demonstrated that the stereotypical image of black America being fed to it by the media was, at best, incomplete and, at worst, demeaning. In addition, *The Cosby Show* also transformed poorly rated NBC into the leading television network, and it helped establish Thursday nights as its stronghold of "must see" TV.

By late 1987, Bill Cosby, star of TV, films, comedy albums, and the stand-up comedy circuit, had achieved everything in his career that Adam Sandler was only just setting out to do. So, when Lorenzo Quinn introduced Adam to Cosby, the budding comedian was understandably nervous at meeting this legendary talent.

Having Cosby, an expert stand-up comic, ask to see his routine did not make Sandler any less tense. As reported by Nancy West in Manchester, New Hampshire's *Union Leader* (December 3, 1987), Cosby sat stone-faced through Adam's performance— and afterward offered him four simple words of advice: "Clean up your act!"

Adam took Bill Cosby's sage advice to heart. Over the next several months, he toned down his material—and soon after, the effort started paying results. The first of those was the acquisition of a manager.

It should be remembered that, in the late 1980s, comedy was dominated by crude. Eddie Murphy's *Raw* album and concert videotape were riding triumphant, and Andrew Dice Clay was also at the height of his foul-mouth popularity.

When Lucien Hold, who then, as now, was responsible for booking one of New York's top stand-up showcases, the Comic Strip, first saw Sandler perform, the young comedian's act (Cosby-inspired) struck him as a breath of fresh air. Adam's routines were (relatively) clean, and his onstage demeanor was basically appealing.

Hold alerted Richie Tienken, one of the owners of the Comic Strip, to the young talent's promise. Tienken, who had managed Eddie Murphy early in the *SNL* comic's career, now signed on to do the same type of representation for Sandler.

The first thing Tienken did was to arrange for his new client to audition for Barry Moss, head of Hughes-Moss Casting, who, in a stroke of serendipity, turned out to be the casting director for *The Cosby Show*. Moss was also won over by Sandler's act and joined as co-manager. He then turned right around and secured a part for his new client on television's number one comedy.

Adam's first appearance on *The Cosby Show* was on December 3, 1987, in the episode "Dance Mania," where he had the small part of "Todd." Having come through the appearance unscathed, for the next week's installment ("The Locker Room") the sitcom's scripters created the character of Smitty for Sandler.

It was a role geared to emphasize Adam's strengths. Smitty was a friend of Cosby's on-air son Theo—played by actor Malcolm Jamal-Warner. Smitty's biggest part came in the March 23, 1988, episode entitled "The Prom."

In that installment—the next to last entry of the show's fourth season—Theo and Smitty are trying to impress their prom dates. They originally plan to hire a limousine from Smitty's uncle—but then decide that arriving in a helicopter would make an even bigger impression on the girls. After a series of mishaps, they rent a helicopter—which, of course, leads to disaster. The wind generated by the blades ruins their dates' hairdos, and by the time they land at the prom, they've missed the entire big event.

Adam's oncamera work impressed the producers of *The Cosby Show*. As a result Sandler would appear on a few other episodes of the highly popular TV series. Meanwhile, Sandler's equally enthusiastic managers proceeded to get their young client his first exposure to the audience that would eventually make him a superstar.

New York–based MTV was hardly the cultural phenomenon in the 1980s that it is today. Back then, the cable network had no shows such as *Real World, Road Rules, Undressed,* or *Loveline.* There were no annual MTV Movie Awards, no *House of Style,* and certainly no *Beavis & Butthead.* The cable channel was devoted to "music television." Besides repeats of British comedy shows such as *The Young Ones* and *Monty Python's Flying Circus,* MTV's programming consisted of VJs (television's answer to radio's disc jockeys) playing music videos. Those VJs filmed their segments not in a Times Square studio surrounded by hordes of screaming teenagers, but locked away in an old warehouse in the borough of Queens. It wasn't until December 7, 1987, that MTV broadcast its first original non-music program. It was a half-hour game show called *Remote Control*.

Hosted by Ken Ober, each episode featured three contestants, who lay back in La-Z-Boy chairs—in a funky basement playroom setting—watching televisions tuned to channels featuring 1970s sitcoms such as *The Brady Bunch* and *The Partridge Family*. The object of the game? Contestants were to respond to pop-culture questions concerning those bygone shows, using their remote controls to click whenever they thought they had the right answer.

Remote Control served as the prototype for the MTV game-show format later utilized by *Singled Out* and *Love Connection*. There was a host (Ober), an announcer (Colin Quinn, who would later go on to be a *Saturday Night Live* repertory player), and a variety of sidekicks: actor/comedian Denis Leary, actress Kari Wuhrer (*Sliders*), and a young Adam Sandler.

"[Adam] did two very, very funny characters," recalled Milton Lage, the show's director, in a March 1999 interview with Chris Koseluk of the *Hollywood Reporter*. "One was Stick Pin Quinn, Colin Quinn's [supposed] cousin, and the other was Stud Boy. . . . I would be in the control room cutting [between] the cameras. It was difficult to do my job when Adam came out because I'd be laughing so hard."

As "Stud Boy," Adam's on-air role was to make statements about his relationship(s) with an unnamed television star of the opposite sex, who the contestants would then have to identify. Over the next several months on this thirty-minute show, Adam claimed to have been Bea Arthur's (*Maude*) boyfriend, spied on "Weezie" Jefferson (*The Jeffersons*) in her bathtub, been given a tingle by the "ebony goddess" Robin Givens, and been yearned after by then-British Prime Minister Margaret Thatcher. The outrageous character captivated the MTV audience, and the showcase gave Adam his first taste of fame. Kids on the streets of Greenwich Village recognized him as "Stud Boy," an experience he'd return to his dorm room and share with Herlihy and his other college buddies. *Remote Control* even went on tour for a few weeks—giving Adam a preview of what life on the road would later be like.

"That was a great time. . . . We did all these colleges," Sandler told writer Betsy Pickle of the *Knoxville* (Tennessee) *News-Sentinel* in 1994. "We'd come on stage and the place was so excited, and it was, like, these big auditoriums. . . . I just felt a little bit like what a rock 'n' roll guy would feel."

More MTV appearances followed in the late 1980s: "Full-time" student Adam co-hosted a few of the cable channel's first *Spring Break* shows and was also a frequent performer on the *MTV Half-Hour Comedy Hour*. His stand-up from this period is incredibly uneven, with lack of planning being the major cause. Adam was not the type of comedian who prepared meticulously for his performances. He'd often just wing it. Despite the years of experience he'd had performing by this point, Sandler still wasn't entirely comfortable onstage. Watching tapes of these early shows, though, you can see his comedic persona begin to emerge: He's obnoxious, self-deprecating, and more than a little unsure oncamera around girls. One of his often-repeated sketches of the time involved a surefire way to get free drinks at a bar—insult women customers and egg them on to throw drinks in his face.

As Adam would later tell MTV's Chris Connelly in June 1999, "I was terrible. But . . . I had something in my mind that was making me do it." Sandler's drive was seemingly inexhaustible: At one point, he was working the Comic Strip virtually every night of the week—while ostensibly attending school full-time.

And if he wasn't exactly blowing away the audience, he was definitely learning his craft.

"With Adam it was never about the material, he was just so likeable," Lucien Hold, the Comedy Strip's booker, told writer Tom Green (*USA Today*) in April 1994. "He was onstage for fifteen minutes, and he had only told two jokes, and the audience was laughing hysterically," recalled Ozzy, the Comic Strip's former doorman, in a November 30, 1988, article in *People* magazine.

Perhaps the best thing that happened to Adam during his stand-up performances occurred not during, but after one of his shows: He met Margaret Ruden, a young cosmetics industry executive. The twentysomething Ruden and Adam were soon involved in a serious romantic relationship, one that would last close to six years and take them to the brink of the altar.

With his stand-up career catching fire, his *Cosby Show* and MTV appearances under his belt, the next logical step for Adam was a move out West. Putting his studies at NYU on hold (he would eventually graduate in 1991, with a Bachelor of Fine Arts degree), Sandler moved out to Los Angeles, renting an apartment with writer/NYU pal Judd Apatow, who was also looking to break into the entertainment business.

Their buddy Jack Giarraputo followed shortly thereafter.

"Jack came to visit for a week," actress Leslie Mann—Apatow's girlfriend at the time, and now his wife—later recalled to writer Stephen Schaefer in a June 1999 piece for the *Boston Herald*. "And stayed six months on the couch!"

Having his old friends around to hang out with was nice: Adam soon made a few new ones as well.

San Francisco native Rob Schneider had spent several years doing stand-up in the clubs and cafes that dotted the Bay City's Haight-Ashbury neighborhood before moving south to Los Angeles. He and Adam met while performing in clubs in Los Angeles, and soon realized they lived within a few miles of each other, as did another young comedian, David Spade.

"We hung out and did stand-up and tried to make each other laugh," Spade said in a 1992 interview with *Inside Media*'s Ed Martin. "It was a fun ride."

The ride also included Adam's motion picture debut. In 1989, he appeared in *The Unsinkable Shecky Moskowitz* (the film's working title only: It's now available in video stores as *Going Overboard,* and occasionally, as *Babes Ahoy*). With a title like that, you would not expect a work of cinematic genius . . . and you'd be right.

Shot almost entirely on a cruise ship bound from New Orleans to Cancun, the beach resort in southeast Mexico, the movie focused on a vessel filled with beauty queens from all over the United States on their way to the Miss Universe Pageant. To use the very words of Sandler's character from the picture, this screen project wasn't "a low-budget affair, it's a no-budget affair." The production crew, for example, forgot an entire box of camera lenses, so the director of cinematography was forced to shoot with the wrong ones for most sequences.

In this movie, Adam plays Shecky Moskowitz, a waiter on the cruise ship, whose dream is to become a successful stand-up comedian. For much of the R-rated proceedings, he's forced to endure the insults of the crew, passengers, and ship's comedian Dicky Diamond. With encouragement from the ship's bartender (played by his NYU buddy Allen Covert), Milton Berle (as himself), and King Neptune (Billy Zane of future *Titanic* fame, in a bizarre cameo appearance), Shecky finally overcomes his self-doubt ("standing up on stage alone is one of the most pathetic things in the world") and performs for the passengers aboard. For good measure, throw into the mix a disheveled General Noriega (played by character actor Burt Young, best known for his role in the *Rocky* movies and as Rodney Dangerfield's chauffeur in 1986's *Back to School*), a rehabbing rock star (portrayed by the film's co-producer, Adam Rifkin), and two bumbling assassins who, by the end of the movie, become stand-up comics themselves. The result is a movie that, to put it charitably, does not hold up to repeat viewings.

The Unsinkable Shecky Moskowitz was never released theatrically; it went straight to video, courtesy of TriMark distributors. In a review of the ninety-eight-minute movie for the online site *Bad Movie Night,* Jason Coffman called it "the worst film I have ever seen." The site uses a rating system based on beans, not stars: The more beans a film gets, the worse it is. Ten beans is the lowest rating a movie can receive.

"I give this film ten beans," said Coffman. "Only because I cannot give it fifteen."

Actress Valerie Breiman, who made her directorial debut on this movie, is also credited as the film's writer. Sandler's creative hand is everywhere, however, in the self-doubt his character feels, in the song his character sings, in the jokes he tells during his stand-up routine. In his white waiter's uniform, close-cut dark hair, and what remains of his childhood overbite, Sandler resembles the young Jerry Lewis in *Cinderfella* (1960).

Besides Burt Young and Billy Zane, other familiar faces in the would-be comedy are Billy Bob Thornton (a later Oscar nominee for his work in 1996's *Sling Blade*), a virtually unrecognizable Peter Berg (the future Dr. Billy Kronk on CBS-TV's *Chicago Hope*) who plays the manager of rock star Adam Rifkin, and Zane's then-wife, actress Lisa Collins, seen as "Miss Australia."

In addition to his acting duties in his debut feature, Adam also performed two musical numbers, which appeared as part of the film's background music: a laid-back version of Bachman-Turner Overdrive's "You Ain't Seen Nothin' Yet," and a surprisingly straight reading of the Temptations' classic "Just My Imagination."

Going Overboard—to put it mildly—didn't exactly fulfill Adam's movie-star dreams.

Luckily, good things were happening at his comedy club stand-up performances.

He was working clubs on both coasts now to increasing crowds and show-business buzz. Adam was also beginning to attract a sizeable female contingent to his shows.

"He had this really innocent look," recalled Jamie Masada, owner of the Los Angeles comedy club The Laugh Factory, in a March 1999 interview with the *Hollywood Reporter*'s Chris Koseluk. Masada remembers that Sandler had "this onstage huggable quality. He could do something really crazy and no one would become hostile toward him. Everyone wanted to be his friend. Girls said they wanted to take him home."

Other now-familiar faces on the stand-up circuit at that time included Schneider, Spade, Chris Rock, and New Jersey native Jon Stewart. In a 1999 interview with writer Eric Layton of *Entertainment Today*, Stewart—now the host of Comedy Central's *The Daily Show*—recalled being impressed (and depressed) while watching Adam's act.

"[Adam] and Chris Rock started around the same time as I did, and they made me feel bad, because I was older. I thought, *These two young punks are gonna have no trouble at all, and it's really annoying.*"

Stewart was right: In the summer of 1990, both Adam and Chris were asked to join the staff of *Saturday Night Live.*

One rumor has it that it was a performance at the Improv, a popular West Hollywood club on Sunset Boulevard, that established comedian Dennis Miller caught that won Adam the TV job. Another rumor is that *Saturday Night Live* creator/executive producer Lorne Michaels saw Sandler humping a chair during his club act, and hired him.

The truth, in fact, was much less colorful. Sandler's managers had worked overtime to secure him an audition for the legendary TV show. They flew him to Chicago, where *SNL*'s producers had set up a showcase for several young comics (including Chris Rock).

The normally improvisational Sandler worked overtime to make sure he was ready for the test, going so far as to actually write an outline for his entire act. The night before, alone in his hotel room, Adam steeled himself for the performance.

"I remember looking in the mirror," he told Chris Connelly of MTV, "thinking 'come on man—you better not choke.'"

He didn't. As casting director Barry Moss later told freelance journalist Jon Salem (for that author's 1999 book, *Adam Sandler,*

Not Too Shabby), "He was incredible. It might have been the best stand-up Adam's ever done."

A few days later word came through that Adam had gotten the job. He would be joining *Saturday Night Live* for its 1990–91 TV season.

At the age of twenty-four, Adam Sandler's dreams were fast beginning to take professional shape.

CHAPTER 4

the big break

"You look up 'break' in the dictionary, and for a comedian,

it says, 'see Saturday Night Live.'*"*

COMEDIAN/ACTOR DANA CARVEY, 1989

BACK WHEN ART DECO WAS THE NEWEST STYLE, when Frank Sinatra was the reigning teen heartthrob and Jack Benny was the reigning King of Comedy, when television was a luxury and the train was every American's preferred method of travel, NBC—a radio network in those days—broadcast its premier shows out of their studios in the RCA building, in the heart of Rockefeller Center in midtown Manhattan. One of those studios—number 8-H—was constructed in grand style, specifically for the prestigious NBC Symphony's radio broadcasts, then being conducted by the legendary Italian conductor Arturo Toscanini. At more than eight thousand square feet, the room comfortably held a complete orchestra, the conductor, and room for the network's broadcast facilities. When NBC metamorphosed into a commercial TV network in the late 1940s, the weekly *Kraft Television Theatre* (1947–54) was aired from there.

Today, Toscanini, Benny, and Sinatra are gone; the RCA building has been renamed by NBC's new corporate parent, General Electric, and practically no one uses the railroad. But studio 8-H remains. Since 1975, approximately twenty-two Saturdays per year, that studio (with Toscanini's podium relocated to the announcer's booth) has played host to what is arguably the most influential television program of the last twenty-five years—the late night comedy/variety series *Saturday Night Live*.

Even in 1990, fans of *Saturday Night Live* were splitting the show's lengthy run into several distinct eras. First was 1975–80: the reign of the original Not Ready For Prime Time Players, including the previously mentioned Dan Aykroyd, Gilda Radner, John Belushi, Jane Curtin, Chevy Chase, and so on. Next came the period bounded roughly by the years 1981–85. The most prominent cast members from this time were Eddie Murphy and Joe Piscopo. In 1986, a third regime started, which included cast members Dana Carvey, Phil Hartman, Jon Lovitz, and Dennis Miller.

For the 1990–91 TV season, the show's creator/executive producer Lorne Michaels deliberately sought out fresh faces to perk up the fare. To returning cast members Dana Carvey, Phil Hartman, Jan Hooks, Victoria Jackson, Dennis Miller, Mike Myers, and Kevin Nealon, he added a group of young talent including Chris Farley, Tim Meadows, Chris Rock, Rob Schneider, David Spade, Julia Sweeney . . . and Adam Sandler.

One can imagine the cheering in the Sandler family's Manchester, New Hampshire, home, the smiles on the faces of his old college buddies, and the pride his girlfriend Margaret Ruden must have felt, when they learned of Adam's good career fortune.

One can also imagine Adam feeling a bit disappointed that he was being asked to join *SNL not* as a performer, but as a writer. "I didn't even know I knew how to write," Adam would later tell *Drama-Logue*'s Elias Stimac, in a February 1998 interview, "but I thought, *That's the place I want to be, SNL. And maybe I'll start writing myself into scenes.*"

Adam moved back to New York City. He found an apartment a few blocks from *SNL*'s offices at 30 Rockefeller Plaza, and crammed into a work space with fellow new hirees: diminutive David Spade and oversized Chris Farley.

There was work—a lot of work—to be done.

The first thing to realize about *SNL* is that it is a live ninety-minute television show, put together by writers, contributing cast members, and a production staff within the space of a Monday to Saturday work week. That meant the program's several sketches had to be conceived, written and rewritten, rehearsed, and appropriate props and sets designed and constructed, within the span of six hectic days. It was a high-pressure environment, an insane, hectic schedule that saw cast and crew alike routinely pulling all-nighters to complete their tough weekly assignments.

But that continuous high pressure had forged stars—actors who had gone on to conquer not just the small screen, but

Hollywood as well. And although critics often carped at their work, the moviegoing public embraced films like *The Blues Brothers* (1980), *National Lampoon's Vacation* (1983), *Ghostbusters* (1984), *Beverly Hills Cop* (1984), and, of course, Adam's beloved *Caddyshack* (1980). These and other screen comedies made movie stars out of many *SNL* repertory players. Becoming one of those future big screen luminaries was certainly on the minds of every one of *SNL's* new "featured players."

But with the addition of that crop of new talent on *SNL*, available onscreen time became much harder to come by, not just for the comedians, but also for the writers. This was the time of Dana Carvey's "Church Lady," of the bodybuilding duo Hans and Franz, of Garth and Wayne from "Wayne's World": Any new characters would gain exposure only at the expense of those established repertory characters and other returning audience favorites.

Rob Schneider hit the jackpot almost immediately on *SNL* with the "copy-machine guy"—a nondescript office worker who sat near the company Xerox machine and annoyed his co-workers by incorporating their names into ridiculous phrases.

Schneider's success was the opening salvo in what would become, over the next decade, a friendly game of comic "one-upmanship" between *SNL's* young guns—Sandler, Chris Farley, Chris Rock, Schneider, and David Spade—all competing in a madcap race for TV success. It truly was a rivalry that engendered no ill will, however, as is witnessed by the fact that Adam is currently acting as executive producer (and driving force) behind Rob Schneider's first starring film venture, *Deuce Bigalow: Male Gigolo* (1999).

Adam's onscreen TV debut finally took place on the December 9, 1990, episode hosted by Tom Hanks. That installment is best-remembered now for its "Five-Timers" sketch—where Hanks is seen being welcomed into an exclusive club for celebrities (Steve Martin, Elliott Gould, and Paul Simon, who all play themselves) who had, as the sketch's title implies, already hosted the show five times. (When viewing reruns of this *SNL* show, in this skit watch for a cameo by then *SNL* staff writer, Conan O'Brien, as the club's doorman.)

On this December 1990 edition of *Saturday Night Live,* a very nervous Adam appeared in a skit with Tom Hanks. Sandler played a native-born Israeli—"I can do an Israeli accent," he would tell writer Ruthe Stein of the *San Francisco Chronicle* in February 1996—who is appearing on a home shopping channel.

"[I remember] sitting with Tom Hanks ten seconds before the lights come up," he told Kevin Cook in a February 1999 interview with *Playboy* magazine. "I said, 'I might faint. There is a good chance I'm going to faint.' Hanks looks over, real concerned, and says, 'Well, don't.'"

Adam didn't. His nervousness didn't fade all that quickly, though.

"[When] I began to get one-liners on the show, I'd rehearse all week. I thought it was a now-or-never thing," he told writer Mal Vincent in a 1994 interview for the *Norfolk Virginian-Pilot.* "I'd go over and over that one line right up until air time. I was actually surprised when no one paid any attention."

Most notable among Adam's other 1990–91 *SNL* appearances was his role as "Iraqi Pete," a character who spews forth anti-American invective during the early days of the Gulf War. "We got a lot of hate mail about that," Sandler told Ed Martin (*Inside Media*) during a 1992 interview. As a result, this character never appeared again on the TV series.

During *SNL*'s summer hiatus in 1991, Adam focused on acting opportunities. He played a minor role (Dink the clown) in *Shakes the Clown* (1991) directed by and starring eccentric comedian Bob Goldthwait. Concerned with the (mis)adventures of an alcoholic clown (Goldthwait), the R-rated film's unquestioned high points were uncredited appearances by Robin Williams and Florence Henderson. Also during the *SNL* off season, Adam managed to squeeze in an appearance on the 1991 *ABC Afterschool Special*, "Testing Dirty." The installment went on to win a DGA Award for director Lynn Hamrick.

The *SNL* break also provided Adam with a chance to kick back and absorb the sights and sounds of New York City. Like any good comedian, he always has had keen eyes for the eccentric, and the rich and varied street life he observed would provide him with plenty of raw material for his upcoming second season with *Saturday Night Live*.

The passing of the talent torch anticipated by Lorne Michaels began to occur in *SNL*'s 1991–92 season. Long-time cast members Dennis Miller and Jan Hooks left the show: Chris Farley, Chris Rock, and Julia Sweeney were promoted to the repertory troupe to replace them. Adam was formally added to the list of featured players, along with newcomers Beth Cahill, Ellen Cleghorne, Siobhan Fallon, and Melanie Hutsell.

Right from the very first episode (September 21, 1991) of the season (hosted by athlete Michael Jordan), Adam made an impression with home viewers. He and Chris Farley debuted in one of the year's most memorable sketches: their "commercial" for Schmitt's Gay Beer. It was in the tradition of *SNL* classics like Dan Aykroyd's ad lampoon for "Del Stater's Rabbit Hut" (where you selected the rabbit you wanted to eat, and watched as it was killed, cooked, and delivered to your table). The Gay Beer commercial savagely lampooned the beer advertisements of that time, which always seemed to feature fetching young women gathered around a swimming pool. In Sandler and Farley's take, of course, the nubile bodies belonged to buff young men: The two comedians are seen happily frolicking with their "guests," repeatedly high-fiving each other over their "score."

Adam also became a familiar face—actually, *several* familiar faces—on the "Weekend Update" segment of the TV series. One of *SNL*'s most popular features since its inception, the Update skit was devoted to a satirical take of a typical TV news program. It was centered around the fictional news program's anchor— a role first portrayed by Chevy Chase, then Bill Murray, Dennis Miller, and (for most of Adam's tenure on *SNL*) Kevin Nealon. The anchor poked fun at, parodied, and savagely dissected the week's current events, depending on the particular performer's strength.

The 1991–92 season was Nealon's first as replacement for Dennis Miller as the sketch's anchor. Where Miller had been all caustic wit and sarcasm, Nealon was more subdued, letting the parodies speak for themselves—which worked perfectly against the eccentric cast of characters Adam created that year for *SNL*.

The first of Adam's comic creations to take the Update desk next to Nealon was "Cajunman." Based on a restaurant patron Sandler and his friends had encountered during an evening out in New York (an out-of-towner who kept insisting he and his party had a 'reserva-TION'), Cajunman came dressed in overalls, a sleeveless flannel shirt, and a straw hat. More than anything else, though, what distinguished the character was Sandler's ever-present grin—which he always seemed to make just a bit broader when giving his one-word answers to anchorman Nealon's questions, as if egging the audience on. Every one of those terse responses, ended in the accented suffix "TION"—for example, "sta-TION," "na-TION," "inspec-TION," and so on.

Actually, the Nealon/Cajunman exchanges on air were rarely about news items: The anchor inquired after Cajunman's mood ("depres-SION"), his choice of beer ("Pabst Blue Rib-BON"), his love life ("rejec-TION"), and even his body odor ("on-ION"). Other memorable Sandler appearances from the 1991–92 season would include a dead-on impersonation of Axl Rose (the lead singer of Guns 'n' Roses), the first of his cheap Halloween costume tips segments, and, late in the year, the character he would become best known for: "Operaman."

In the 1994 book *Saturday Night Live: The First Twenty Years,* the fast-rising comic talked about that character's genesis with that tome's editor, Michael Cader.

"[There was] a guy on Fifty-seventh Street. . . [he] sings opera and gets money in a cup. I just used to do impressions of him, and the Turners [*SNL* staff writers Bonnie and Terry] made it into an Update."

What the Turners did was use Adam's impression—and his impressive vocal and facial gesture skills—to create a memorable character who provided yet another take on the current news. Dressed in a full cape, tuxedo with bow tie, and a wig with shoulder-length, straight dark hair, Adam-as-Operaman would appear at the Update desk next to Kevin Nealon and burst into frequent song filled with barb-filled, rhyming lyrics.

Operaman was arguably the season's most popular new character, while, without a doubt, *Il Cantore,* a sketch about an Italian restaurant's over-amorous staff that Adam and Rob Schneider co-wrote, was its most controversial.

A word about censorship on *SNL:* Ever since the TV show's early days in the mid-1970s, when writers such as Dan Aykroyd, John Belushi, and Michael O'Donoghue pushed the envelope of what was then permitted on prime-time network television, the censors have kept a close watch on the program. With the advent of more permissive cable TV, and with broadcast shows such as *NYPD Blue* (1993–present) routinely featuring partial nudity and off-color language that would have gotten Lorne Michaels fired back in the 1970s, the bar has been somewhat lowered. The censors, however, still have hot buttons that can be pushed. The *SNL* producers have to be sensitive to their advertisers' concerns as well—and all involved must be very careful about drawing the ire of any particular special interest group. What troubles sponsors, interest groups, and censors more than anything else are matters of sex and things related to that controversial subject—all of which the *Il Cantore* sketch had in abundance.

The piece started simply enough: A husband and wife couple, played by that week's (October 12, 1991) host Kirstie Alley (*Cheers, Veronica's Closet*) and Kevin Nealon, dine at an Italian restaurant. They're warmly greeted by maitre d' Dana Carvey, who proceeds to shake Nealon's hand and give Alley a very enthusiastic kiss, all the while mumbling sweet Italian nothings to her.

Shown to their table, Kirstie is further treated to a very enthu-siastic reception (which includes various acts of nuzzling/fondling/groping) by Carvey's character and several of his restaurant co-workers, including Rob Schneider and Sandler. Adam's char-acter goes so far as to strip down to his underwear oncamera and bury his face in Alley's breasts.

What got the sketch in trouble though, was not what was happening at Alley and Nealon's table, but at the table behind them. There, cast member Victoria Jackson was lying on her back, legs spread wide, while Dana Carvey stood above her, simu-lating "the act of love." The censors watching the skit rehearsal took one look at Carvey's pumping motions and declared those movements inappropriate: They had to be cut from the sketch before it actually aired.

As Adam told *Inside Media*'s writer Ed Martin in May 1992, there's a very specific chain of command between the *SNL* staff and the network censors. Instructions about what to delete from a particular scene are relayed first to the show's producer, who then passes the demands on to the sketch's writer(s), who then (finally) advise(s) the performers of the changes they must make before the live performance in front of the studio audience.

The first chance the censors get to see the show's planned material is generally during the dress rehearsal, which occurs Saturday evening at 7:30 P.M.—just four short hours before *SNL* goes on the air. It's a hectic time: Camera angles, staging, and sketch order are still being evaluated; performers, prop artists, and production personnel are running about the stage. Literally a million little details are being ironed out.

Needless to say, the cast members have a lot on their collec-tive minds.

When one of the censors approached Adam and told him about the changes he needed to have Dana make during the *Il Cantore* sketch, Adam readily agreed.

"But it was so crazy," Adam recalled. "I was performing, doing other things. . . . I didn't see Dana [Carvey]; he had so many makeup changes and stuff. I remember, it was like Five, Four, Three. . . . Dana! Dana! I'm trying to tell him 'Don't pump! Don't pump!'"

Busily performing for the live audience, Carvey couldn't understand what Sandler was trying to say: The sketch—and Dana's motions—went forward on the air just as they had in rehearsal.

"The next day a big note was on my desk. 'Adam Sandler is in trouble.'"

Not too much trouble, as it turned out: Lorne Michaels stood up to the network censors for Sandler, as he had for so many others in previous seasons. The controversy soon faded.

Overall, *SNL*'s 1991–92 season was one of the show's strongest in recent years: The series' Nielsen home viewer ratings jumped about 12 percent, from a 7.4 to an 8.3. As a further testament to the show's quality, Michaels was honored as Broadcaster of the Year by the International Radio and Television Society.

Perhaps the most important *SNL*-related event of 1992, however, occurred not on the small screen, but on the big one.

The movie *Wayne's World,* based on the long-running *SNL* sketch with Mike Myers and Dana Carvey, was released in February 1992 by Paramount Pictures. Co-produced by Lorne Michaels, the major motion picture took in $183 million worldwide and proved that the marketplace was ripe for feature films starring the newest era of *SNL* comedians.

It would be several more years before Adam was ready to enter this big league at full steam. During the 1992 summer hiatus, however, he continued to test the Hollywood waters, gaining valuable experience on the way. Along with fifteen other *SNL* regulars, past and present (in alphabetical order—Dan Aykroyd, Peter Aykroyd, Jane Curtin, Tom Davis, Chris Farley, Phil Hartman, Jan Hooks, Jon Lovitz, Michael McKean, Tim Meadows, Garrett Morris, Kevin Nealon, Larraine Newman, David Spade, and Julia Sweeney), Sandler had a small role in the 1993 Paramount Pictures release *Coneheads*. (The number of ex-*SNL*ers in the film would have been even greater, but scenes with Ellen Cleghorne, Brian Doyle-Murray, and Conan O'Brien were cut at the last minute.)

Derived from the *SNL* sketch of the same name, the PG-rated movie, directed by Steve Barron, starred Dan Aykroyd and Jane Curtin as married aliens with cone-shaped heads . . . posing as immigrants from France. Adam's character in the movie, Carmine, attempts to help the aliens get the necessary legal papers to stay in the United States.

Adam's appearance in the eighty-eight-minute *Coneheads* amounted to little more than a cameo. Meanwhile, Sandler's *SNL* "rival," Rob Schneider, was receiving acclaim for his role in *Home Alone 2: Lost in New York* (1992) and had already been cast for parts in the big-screen remake of *The Beverly Hillbillies* (1993) and the low-budget comedy *Surf Ninjas* (1993).

In the friendly competition between those two comedians, it was clear Schneider was now winning the race by a landslide.

Even Pauly Shore, who in a sense had replaced Adam on MTV as the cable channel's "bad boy" (having become a major on-air personality for the network by the early 1990s), was already headlining his own movies, such as 1992's *Encino Man*.

Yet, although there may have been some frustration on the ever-ambitious Sandler's part at seeing his contemporaries get more time on the big screen, Adam was very comfortable proceeding at his own career pace. In a very real sense, he was doing the same thing with film he had done with stand-up comedy—learning his craft slowly but surely.

"*SNL* was our boot camp for movies," he would later tell MTV's Chris Connelly in mid-1999. "You would produce your own piece. . . . You would help tell the actors in your skit how you wanted it to be; you'd talk to the director about what kind of shots you want. That prepared [me] for movie-making."

Adam also spent part of the *SNL* summer hiatus doing stand-up: In July 1992, he played Montreal's "Just for Laughs" comedy festival with one of his childhood idols, veteran funster Jerry Lewis.

Back to work at *SNL* as the 1992–93 season opened on September 26, 1992, with movie star Nicolas Cage as guest host, Adam returned to substantially the same lineup of players: Victoria Jackson was the only cast member to jump ship, Beth Cahill and Siobhan Fallon the only featured players to leave the program. Though Adam remained in the program's supporting player category, his popularity—and on-air time—was growing.

Adam's Operaman returned during the new *SNL* season, as did his Halloween costume tips. He, David Spade, and Chris Farley debuted the Gap Girls skit, where store clerks Lucy (Sandler), Cindy (Farley), and Christy (Spade), in a savage parody of the retail chain's seemingly endless supply of apparently clueless young clerks, debate such crucial topics as whether Rwanda is a nightclub or a country.

In addition, Adam demonstrated his skills as an impersonator in the series's new season. He did a dead-on imitation of Bill Cosby mumbling his way through an episode of the classic game show *You Bet Your Life* (which his former comic adviser had unwisely revived during the 1992–93 TV season), donned a wig and sunglasses to play a stoned-looking Pauly Shore in a parody of MTV's *Spring Break,* and reprised his Axl Rose impression, singing in the "Musicians for Free-Range Chicken Benefit" sketch.

Adam's vocal talent became an increasingly indispensable part of his on-air shtick: More and more, people knew him for his oncamera song renditions. He vocalized on air a self-penned tune called "I Love You, Momma" during a Mother's Day "Weekend Update" segment; on another Update appearance, he sang "Red-Hooded Sweatshirt," with Linda and Paul McCartney providing backup harmonies.

With his singing skills receiving such a showcase, the next natural career goal for the twenty-six-year-old comedian seemed to be to make a hit record.

○   ○   ○

Adam began shopping the idea of an album based on his act in early 1993. In negotiating with record labels, he made it clear that his material—which presented a much cruder, ruder, more sophomoric version than the Adam *SNL* viewers were accustomed to seeing—was intended not for them or their peers, but for college-age kids. "I don't expect you to get it," he said. "But the fans will."

Warner Bros. executive Lenny Waronker was impressed by Sandler's presentation—"He knew what he wanted to do and how to do it"—and signed Adam to a label contract on the spot.

Recorded on a shoestring budget at New York City's The Hit Factory, the album was produced by music business veteran Brooks Arthur—who'd worked with performers from the Shangri-Las and Neil Diamond to Van Morrison and Janis Ian. Though it was his first comedy album, Arthur took the identical approach to working with Sandler as he had with previous projects. "It's the same as producing singers," Arthur told the music industry magazine *Studio Sound* in May 1998. "It's all about performance, and knowing how to capture [it]."

Helping Adam nail down his performance were his buddies past and present, including Tim Herlihy and Margaret Ruden, as well as *SNL*'s Rob Schneider, David Spade, Tim Meadows, Robert Smigel, and Conan O'Brien.

Released in September of 1993, the album, titled *They're All Gonna Laugh at You,* presented the uncensored, unbridled Sandler, in a format that young America—in particular, teenage boys—responded to immediately.

And no wonder. With cuts such as "The Beating of a High School Janitor," "The Beating of a High School Bus Driver," "The Beating of a High School Science Teacher," "The Beating of a High School Spanish Teacher," and "The Longest Pee," the album was perfectly geared to its target demographic.

They're All Gonna Laugh at You spent more than 100 weeks—two years—on *Billboard* magazine's Heatseekers chart (designed to measure the sales of new artists). Two tracks from the record—"The Thanksgiving Song," and "Lunchlady

Land"—became college radio station favorites. The latter number also spawned an animated video that received heavy airplay on MTV.

Not everybody, though, loved what they heard on Sandler's debut album.

"My two sisters and my parents don't even acknowledge [the album]," Adam told the *Asheville* (North Carolina) *Citizen-Times* in February 1995. "My brother and I lived in the same room growing up, so it was the same humor me and him always did in the bedroom. But my sisters are nice girls and they were baffled by it. When my dad's alone, he laughs . . . but in front of my mother, he's going, 'You stupid (expletive).'"

Initially, the record shipped thirteen thousand copies. By 1996, it had gone platinum, achieving sales of more than one million copies. It was nominated for a Grammy in the Best Spoken Comedy Album category. At the March 1, 1995, Awards at the Shrine Auditorium in Los Angeles, however, it was Sam Kinison who won in that category for his Priority label album *Live from Hell*.

Although the success of *Wayne's World* as a feature film and in home video release had demonstrated that there was a new generation of filmgoers eager for movies that reflected their special sense of humor, *They're All Gonna Laugh at You* proved that there was a similarly untapped audience for properly targeted, new comedy albums.

Those young album buyers were Adam Sandler's generation, and the comedian would soon demonstrate to the show business community that he knew their range of tastes far better than anybody else.

CHAPTER 5

great expectations

"I don't like reading bad stuff about [SNL]. . . .

When someone tries to sum up the whole show in one

stupid sentence, it's pretty ridiculous."

ADAM SANDLER, 1994

GOING INTO THE 1993–94 TV SEASON, the future had never seemed brighter for *Saturday Night Live*. Its core of established performers included Phil Hartman, Mike Myers, and Kevin Nealon (returning after a two-year absence). It also had a wealth of younger talent, including Adam, David Spade, Chris Farley, and Rob Schneider, and the series had just enjoyed a year of high critical praise and the highest ratings in its almost two decades of history on the NBC network. Yet there were danger signs clearly on the horizon.

Dana Carvey, who had provided high-profile political humor with his dead-on impersonations of President George Bush and

White House contender Ross Perot, as well as popular characters such as the Church Lady and Garth from *Wayne's World,* had left the show in the middle of the previous season. Adam's good friend Chris Rock was gone too, heading off to the FOX network's comedy sketch show, *In Living Color* (1990–94), for what would prove to be its last season on the air.

SNL's Lorne Michaels had responded to the defections by adding Norm Macdonald, Jay Mohr, and Sarah Silverman as featured players, and elevating Adam, Ellen Cleghorne, Melanie Hutsell, Tim Meadows, and David Spade to full cast members. Michaels further declared that Phil Hartman—whom he referred to as *SNL*'s 'glue'—would now provide the show's comic center.

The biggest changes, however, on the hour-long comedy-variety program occurred behind the camera. Five of the long-running show's seven writers left, including Jack Handy, who was responsible for the popular "Deep Thoughts" segments; Bob Smigel, who went to work on Conan O'Brien's new late-night NBC-TV talk show; and long-time staffers Bonnie and Terry Turner. Head writer/producer Jim Downey hired six new scribes to work on *SNL,* including veteran comedy writer Marilyn Suzanne Miller and three stand-up comics.

The adjustment was not a smooth one, on—or off—the air.

Almost immediately, critics were negative about the "new" *SNL.* Manuel Mendoza of the *Dallas Morning News* called it "poorly written and directionless." For Rob Salem of the *Toronto Star,* the restaffed program was "unfunny" and "overlong." Home viewer ratings suffered: The show dropped 12 percent (from an 8.8 rating to a 7.7) in the Nielsens.

Ironically, the show's high-water mark—*and* its lowest point—both occurred during the March 12, 1994, installment hosted by figure skater Nancy Kerrigan. Kerrigan's eagerly awaited appearance (the show was broadcast shortly after the Tonya Harding conflict) drew the highest single-episode rating in several years. Yet this renewed attention was a double-edged sword. Unfortunately, Kerrigan was not an experienced television performer, and the evening's fare was weak as well.

The criticism quickly got the attention of new NBC president Don Ohlmeyer. The network had taken a lot of heat the previous year for the controversy surrounding the very public battle between David Letterman and Jay Leno to succeed Johnny Carson as host of *The Tonight Show*. Ohlmeyer, himself, was still feeling the pressure, because Letterman's new *Late Show* on CBS-TV was, at the time, a consistent ratings winner in the 11:30 P.M. slot. Now, determined not to damage yet another jewel in NBC's late-night crown, Ohlmeyer issued a very public challenge to Lorne Michaels to quickly bring *SNL* back up to snuff.

Michaels took the challenge—and the implicit rebuke—in stride. In a May 1994 interview with writer Phil Rosenthal of the *Los Angeles Daily News*, Lorne declared he'd been hearing voices of doom from network executives since the end of the show's first year back in June 1976, when Chevy Chase had decided to leave. "I was here in 'the golden years,' and it wasn't so golden all the time. I was hearing 'Saturday Night Dead' from 1976 on. It's never stopped."

Others, however, admitted that the long-term program was suffering through a creative slump. "We were much hotter last year," comedian Phil Hartman confessed to Rosenthal in the same *Los Angeles Daily News* article. The departed Dana Carvey offered one explanation why. "I think *SNL* shines when there's a political or social event they can parody," Carvey told Rob Salem

of the *Toronto Star* in May 1994. "And maybe the news hasn't
fallen quite their way. . . . We had the Clarence Thomas hearings,
the Gulf War, and then of course the election, and the most hys-
terical politician in history, Ross Perot . . . there's a bit of luck
there."

Others pointed to a generation gap between the old-timers
and the new arrivals on *Saturday Night Live*. Featured performer
Al Franken, who had worked on *SNL* since 1979, confessed to
feeling some of that conflict in a 1994 interview with Doug Hill
of the *New York Times*. Franken recalled sometimes being told
"I'm sorry if you don't understand what I'm doing with this
piece, but it's because you're too old. And I'll say, 'Well, no, I
understand perfectly well what you're doing. I just don't think it's
funny.'"

Writer Marilyn Suzanne Miller, who had first worked on *SNL*
during the original "Not Ready for Prime Time" era and had
recently returned, had a different take on the old versus the new
guard on the long-running TV series. She saw some of the new
performers as mere shadows of the outsized personalities who had
made those earlier seasons such memorable ones. "There wasn't
one person here in the old days who didn't have a piercing personality," she told Hill in the same 1994 *New York Times* article.
"These people are low-key—not necessarily timid, but they're
not exuberant."

Producer Jim Downey, who had been with the show since its
second season (1976–77), suggested in the same *New York Times*
piece that *SNL* was becoming a way station for its stable of
comedians. "Nowadays, anyone coming here knows what the
formula is: A couple of hit characters, then you get a movie."
Many critics agreed, pointing to the amount of time former

workhorse Mike Myers was spending on his budding screen career—which, in addition to 1992's *Wayne's World*, included *So I Married an Axe Murderer* (1993), and *Wayne's World 2* (1993). Those same writers also faulted Lorne Michaels for splitting his attention between *SNL* and other projects, which included the new Conan O'Brien NBC-TV chat show, and a recurring role as executive producer for many of the movies that *SNL* cast members, both old and new, were producing in Hollywood.

There were rumors that Ohlmeyer wanted Michaels to dismiss Jim Downey; some sources had Michaels himself leaving the program. In the midst of all the ongoing turmoil, *SNL*'s creator remained seemingly unruffled. "The beating is part of the game," Lorne told Rosenthal of the *Los Angeles Daily News* in May 1994. "If *Saturday Night* hadn't been always beaten up, somehow we wouldn't be what we are now."

What the show was, despite the sagging home viewership, was still the highest-rated late-night program currently on American television. Moreover, despite its wavering level of quality, the show and its players remained a common point of interest in pop culture. As *SNL* troupe member Dana Carvey would reflect to the *Toronto Star* in May 1994: "*Saturday Night Live* is an important institution. The most interesting thing about [it] is that it's talked about so much. . . . It just shows you how invested everyone is in it."

During *SNL*'s troubled 1993–94 TV season, Adam Sandler was one of the few elements of the program that people continued to talk about in a positive way. Show scripter Marilyn Suzanne Miller cited him as one of the few personalities on the show able to "fill up the room" with his comic presence. Critic Manuel Mendoza praised his "Andy Kaufman–like edge."

The show's nineteenth year was a productive one for Adam. With David Spade and Chris Farley, Sandler reprised the popular "Gap Girls" skit. Operaman and Cajunman also returned, as did his ever-popular Halloween costume tips routine. Sandler debuted a new skit, "The Denise Show," in which he played Brian, a young man who starts a cable show devoted to his former girl-friend, the aforementioned Denise (played by Shannen Doherty of *Beverly Hills, 90210* fame.)

Adam also scored heavily with "Canteen Boy"—a character who, in many ways, was the prototype for virtually all of Adam's forthcoming big-screen creations. Canteen Boy was a shy, not especially talented, not particularly adventurous camper who stayed in the Boy Scouts just a little too long. In Scout uniform (complete with short pants and the traditional Scout cap), Adam played the character with a perpetually dazed look on his face.

"The Canteen Boy, the reason you feel bad for him and you can laugh is because he, and I guess a lot of my characters, they don't notice they're getting made fun of," Adam later told writer Chris Willman of the *Los Angeles Times* (July 10, 1994). "They'll say something back that's not that great a quip, but in their mind they won the argument."

In writing the character, Adam tapped into something that the usually cynical Gen-X kids who made up his TV audience hadn't seen before from a comic of their generation. As Lorne Michaels would later tell Adam Goldworm of *Variety*, Sandler let his fans "see right through to his heart."

Adam gave viewers an underdog to root for, making sure that, at the same time, they had something to laugh at. Canteen Boy had to fight through more than his share of improbable situations—most notably, the scoutmaster with a passion for young campers, played with appropriate smarminess by frequent show host Alec Baldwin.

In other installments of *Saturday Night Live,* Adam—of the riveting facial contortions—impersonated a mumbling Bruce Springsteen, a teetotaling Bono (from the rock group U2), and a confused, meandering Bill Cosby. Sandler debuted several new songs during the year on *SNL,* including his first Christmas tune, and serenaded a cafeteria full of dancing food with his own "Lunchlady Land."

They're All Gonna Laugh at You continued its impressive rise up the record charts throughout the 1993–94 *SNL* season. The album reached #131 on *Billboard*'s list of the top 200 albums, and a full year after its release, was still at #6 on the magazine's Heatseekers chart.

Adam continued to hone his stand-up act during breaks from *SNL.* Now, however, he did not have to resort to doing one-nighters at comedy clubs in the greater New York City area. Thanks to his nationwide television exposure and the success of his album, Sandler was now attracting sell-out crowds at college campuses nationwide. He brought along his old NYU buddy Allen Covert to serve as opening act during several of those performances.

The shows were a wild mixture of stand-up and song: Adam's trademark Axl Rose send-up morphed into a hilarious Edith

Bunker (*All in the Family*) impersonation, Chris Farley jumped onstage and donned long yellow latex gloves to play straight man during "Lunchlady Land," and Adam tossed off one-liners ("I've just finished a big book—345 pages. That's a lot of coloring . . . ") that would have done old-timer Henny Youngman proud.

Adam's popularity at times seemed to surprise him—particularly his appeal to young women, who one reviewer reported "swooning" on his arrival onstage. Greeted by cries from the audience of "I love you" and "I want you," Sandler was pleasantly puzzled. The twenty-seven-year-old hardly considered himself a sex symbol: In fact, as he told writer Betsy Pickle of the *Knoxville* (Tennessee) *News-Sentinel* in May 1994, "I see myself as a goofball."

Writer Ariel Levy, in a July 19, 1999, article for *New York* magazine, suggested one possible reason for Adam's growing female audience—in particular, his growing *Jewish* female audience. As *SNL* put Adam's smiling face on television sets nationwide, more and more young Jewish girls had an opportunity to see him. They were captivated.

As one fan told Levy, "I would watch him on *Saturday Night Live,* and my heart would ache. Nobody knows how much it would ache."

Levy goes on to suggest that these girls recognized in Adam's "goofy, self-deprecating humor" the same kind of funny business they'd witnessed at countless bar mitzvahs. Familiarity, in this instance, bred adoration.

Wherever the fans were coming from, and for whatever reason, their presence (in ever-increasing numbers) was noted by show-business insiders. Adam's fans clearly wanted more of him . . . so more of him they would get.

At various times during the year, Adam and David Spade were rumored in the press to be starring in a film adaptation of MTV's popular animated series *The Beavis & Butthead Show* (1993–98). Then, a new rendition of the classic 1960s sitcom *Gilligan's Island* was reported heading for the big screen, with Adam as hapless Gilligan and Chris Farley as the irascible Skipper.

Though neither of those projects came to fruition, before 1994 was out, Adam's growing army of fans would get not one, but two chances to see him on the big screen.

It was to be an experience surprisingly few of them would enjoy.

Though to the outside world, producer Jim Downey's complaint about the *SNL* cast using the show as a springboard to movies may have had the ring of truth, the fact is that it's not quite that easy to get a motion picture made in 1990s Hollywood. A major reason why *Coneheads* (1993) and the two *Wayne's World* (1992, 1993) movies became realities was that they were produced by the experienced team of Bernie Brillstein and Brad Grey. These two powerhouses were among a very few people who, as then–Sony Pictures chairman Peter Guber told writer Alan Citron of the *Los Angeles Times* in November 1992, "manage both talent and productions."

Brillstein was an old-time Hollywood veteran who'd served as executive producer on two of the earliest *SNL* spin-offs, *The Blues Brothers* (1980) and the two *Ghostbusters* movies (1984, 1989). Grey had worked as a concert promoter and produced cable television shows before the two men joined forces in 1985.

Among their *SNL* clients, Brillstein-Grey counted Dennis Miller, Dana Carvey, Mike Myers, Jon Lovitz, Lorne Michaels, and Adam Sandler, who they'd begun handling during *SNL*'s 1991–92 season.

In 1993, Brillstein and Grey helped Adam land parts in two potentially high-profile features. In the first, director Michael Lehmann's *Airheads* (1994), Sandler was cast as Pip, drummer for a dim-witted heavy metal band called the Lone Rangers. The Twentieth Century–Fox release followed the group's misadventures as they reluctantly seize control of a radio station in a misguided attempt to force the station to play their demo tape on the air.

Lehmann, best known for his work on the cult hit *Heathers* (1989), which launched the careers of Shannen Doherty and Christian Slater, and *Hudson Hawk* (1991), which threatened to torpedo Bruce Willis's box-office standing, initially had conceived of Pip—the supposed "cute" member of the band, the one the girls found irresistible—as the typical long-haired rocker. After meeting Adam, though, he rethought the character's screen look.

"We tried the long wig, but it looked like a wig on him," Lehmann told writer Chris Willman of the *Los Angeles Times* in a 1994 interview. "So we shaved his head instead, and we ended up doing things that took away from what would normally be his attractive qualities. But because of his innocent charm, combined with that 'loser' kind of quality . . . it worked. . . . You could believe [it] when people . . . said that girls really liked him."

One of the girls in the plot line who finds Pip attractive is the station's receptionist, Suzzi, played by Nina Siemaszko. In the middle of the tense oncamera goings-on at the radio station, the two end up on the station manager's couch for what would be

Adam's first—and to date, only—onscreen nude scene. The actor was more than a little nervous.

"I'd been putting the scene out of my mind for weeks until the day came I had to do it . . . , " Adam told writer Mal Vincent of the (Norfolk) *Virginian-Pilot* shortly after the film's release. "I had to strip off and do the scene in front of about twenty burly guys. . . . Nina Siemaszko was, well, uh, very helpful, but still . . . " He may have been uncomfortable with his shirt off, but Adam had no reason to be embarrassed: The twenty-seven-year-old Sandler was in good shape. He did (as he later told TV talk show host David Letterman in a June 1999 appearance) have abs—and biceps—fully the equal of any rock drummer's.

Other scenes in the ninety-one-minute *Airheads* came more naturally to Adam, particularly those with Steve Buscemi, who'd been cast as his older brother. The two made an instant connection.

"I remember one scene . . . Buscemi was yellin' at me . . . and I'm just watchin' him, goin' 'What's the matter with Buscemi? Why's he yellin' at me?' So I would laugh, and [director] Michael Lehmann's like, 'Seriously, Adam, don't laugh.' I'd say, 'I know, I know, I know, I know.' And just like, ten in a row, I'd go, 'Hee, hee.'"

Playing the comedy straight by staying in character was something Sandler initially found difficult to do oncamera. Buscemi, a veteran of numerous movies, including *Barton Fink* (1991) and *Reservoir Dogs* (1992), helped; as did Sandler's pal Allen Covert, on board the film venture as one of the cops who surround the radio station. (Chris Farley was also in the cast in a similar law enforcer role.)

The third member of the Lone Rangers metalheads—and the film's top-billed star—was Brendan Fraser, then coming from the films *School Ties* (1992) and *With Honors* (1994). Sandler made a particularly strong impression on Fraser: "You experience Adam. There's 1 and there's 10 and you get 10 all the time. There's no 2 and 9," he told writer Tom Green of *USA Today* (April 8, 1994).

Steve Buscemi would continue to work with Sandler in several other upcoming pictures. The most important connection Adam made during the film, however, was with its producer, Robert Simonds.

A Yale philosophy major, Simonds had started his film career working as an intern for MGM studios back in 1985. His first movie project was John Ritter's *Problem Child* (1990), which he and director Dennis Dugan made for less than $10 million. The comedy went on to gross close to $100 million worldwide, proving to Simonds that movies could be designed and centered around stars. As such, they didn't need big budgets or big effects to appeal to the teenage audience. All they required was the right star and the proper screen vehicle.

Adam Sandler, Simonds came to believe, was just that kind of motion picture star.

Unfortunately, *Airheads* was the completely wrong big screen vehicle. The film opened August 5, 1994, in 1,228 theaters. It quickly sank without much of a trace. What went wrong?

Critical reaction to the movie was mixed. For Mick LaSalle of the *San Francisco Chronicle* the ninety-one-minute feature was, "informed by a real understanding of heavy metal in all its silliness—the lingo, the look, the stage setups, the ridiculous lyrics, the clichéd guitar licks." Leonard Klady of *Daily Variety,* on the other hand, mocked the movie's "slim premise." Richard Harrington of the *Washington Post* found it "fitfully amusing," although Kevin McManus, writing in the same paper, thought *Airheads* was "heavily entertaining."

Adam, too, received both glowing notices and critical brickbats, beginning a tradition that continues to this day. "Sandler breaks through," declared Mal Vincent of the (Norfolk) *Virginian-Pilot.* Not so, according to Owen Gleiberman of *Entertainment Weekly:* "Here, as on *Saturday Night Live,* [Sandler] parades his ironic infantilism." However, for Klady of *Variety,* Adam's performance was right on target as he, "drift[ed] naturally to the required zaniness."

Producer Simonds later pointed to the film's release date as one reason for its box-office failure. "We got cocky and put it in an unsafe corridor, the middle of the summer," he told Bernard Weinraub (*New York Times*) in November 1998. A fair point, considering that 1994 was the summer of *Forrest Gump* and *The Lion King*—two megahits, each of which earned more than $300 million, eventually ending up in the top ten grossing movies of all time. Further competition came from Harrison Ford's new Jack Ryan thriller, *A Clear and Present Danger.* This action movie was released the week before *Airheads,* which undoubtedly grabbed a significant chunk of the latter film's targeted teenage male audience.

Simonds offered journalist Weinraub an additional reason for *Airheads*'s quick demise: "In hindsight, we were basically making fun of the people who were supposed to be coming to see the movie."

Both explanations, however, ignore the unfortunate truth: *Airheads* is simply not a very good movie. Its failure is more accurately attributed to a miscast lead (Brendan Fraser) in a badly conceived hairpiece, and a very uneven script that was given poor pacing onscreen.

Pip, as director Lehmann and Adam shrewdly reconceived the *Airheads* character, is the first big-screen manifestation of Sandler's "loveable loser" persona. For Adam's fans, that's reason enough to see the movie. The film does have other meritorious creative points: A surprisingly believable Joe Mantegna as rebel radio's top DJ, Ian the Shark, a suitably sleazy Judd Nelson as opportunistic record company executive Jimmy Wing, and a very strong soundtrack, including the Lone Rangers's own "D-Generated."

In the end, though, the PG-13-rated *Airheads* grossed less than $6 million.

Adam's first starring role in a major Hollywood feature film was a flop.

○   ○   ○

Adam Sandler had every reason to believe his next movie would be a significantly hotter ticket. TriStar's *Mixed Nuts* (1994) was to be a romantic comedy from the top name (then *and* now) in the screen genre, writer/director Nora Ephron. Fresh from her hit *Sleepless in Seattle* (1993), Nora had decided to adapt the French film *Le Pere Noel Est une Ordure* (1982) into a Hollywood offering, co-writing the screenplay with her sister Delia.

Ephron gathered an all-star cast, headlined by Steve Martin, a frequent *SNL* host and guest performer. Face to face with one of his idols during the film shoot, Adam found himself tongue-tied on the set.

"Steve would ask me a question, and I would just look at his lips moving," Sandler told writer Cindy Pearlman of *Entertainment Weekly* in a piece that appeared on July 29, 1994. "Steve was like, 'It's okay, Adam. You can talk.'"

Others in the stellar troupe included Madeline Kahn, Rita Wilson (Tom Hanks's wife), Rob Reiner, Juliette Lewis, Anthony LaPaglia, Robert Klein, Parker Posey, Jon Stewart, Joely Fisher, Liev Schreiber, Garry Shandling, and, in unbilled roles, Steven Wright and a very young Haley Joel Osmont (the star of 1999's surprise summer hit film, *The Sixth Sense*). Within the ninety-seven-minute plot, all the characters congregate on Christmas Eve, at a Venice, California, suicide hotline center run by Martin, Wilson, and Khan—with one after another mishap occurring.

In this black comedy, Adam is seen as Louie, the center's downstairs neighbor, who has a crush on Wilson's character. To demonstrate his love, Louie serenades her with ballads on his ukulele. Not too surprisingly, Sandler composed those songs himself. (Ephron liked what he was doing so much that she let him improvise additional material.) A good friend of Lorne Michaels, Nora also arranged the movie's shooting schedule so that Adam could film his scenes during breaks from *SNL*.

Mixed Nuts was released at 2,318 theaters in time for Christmas 1994, and the critical (and popular) verdict was unanimous: The PG-13 film should *never* have been made.

It remains inexplicable how so many talented people could come up with such a bad movie. The film is actually painful to watch. Everyone is trying too hard, and nobody seems to be having any fun. As Roger Ebert of the *Chicago Sun-Times*, in giving it half a star (out of four), noted, "Maybe there's too much talent. Every character shines with such dazzling intensity and such inexhaustible comic invention that the movie becomes tiresome, like too many clowns."

Adam's scenes were among the film's most relaxed: His serenades to Wilson and the cross-dressing would-be suicide played by actor Liev Schreiber were, paradoxically enough, the picture's sweetest, most calming moments. (Leonard Klady of *Variety* disagreed, describing Sandler's delivery boy as "just plain irritating.")

Mixed Nuts took in only about $6.6 million, slightly better than *Airheads*, but still an unqualified financial disaster considering its major production values.

After two featured roles in important Hollywood movies, Adam's box-office batting average stood at precisely .000.

He had to be wondering if he'd get another chance at the plate.

Just prior to the release of *Airheads* in mid-1994, Adam Sandler had told reporter Betsy Pickle of the *Knoxville* (Tennessee) *News-Sentinel:* "I hope eventually I can just start acting a lot more. I'm very passionate about what I'm doing and about my comedy and all that. It's the only thing I've ever been passionate about in my life."

All that passion, however, hadn't translated to the screen. In 1994, looking at the box-office totals for Adam's first two important screen releases, a question might legitimately arise whether the audience Adam worked so hard to cultivate (on *SNL*, his comedy album, and his performances) would ever follow him into a movie theater.

Luckily for Adam, another comic actor—one whose career had roughly paralleled his own to that point—was having a much better professional 1994 than he was.

While Adam was becoming one of *Saturday Night Live*'s biggest stars, a young comedian by the name of Jim Carrey was getting noticed for his work on Keenen Ivory Wayans's primetime comedy sketch show, *In Living Color* (1990–94). Canadian-born (1962) Carrey, a few years older than Sandler, had been kicking around Hollywood for a while. He'd had roles in a few pictures (most prominently, 1985's *Once Bitten,* and 1989's *Earth Girls Are Easy*). It was the FOX TV network's *In Living Color* (1990–94), however, with its sketch format, that allowed lanky Jim to stretch creatively in ways that his scripted film roles had not permitted. Carrey brought a manic energy to these TV performances: His most popular character, Fire Marshal Bill, who always went up in a blaze at the end of a skit, also generated some concern. Worried viewers claimed Carrey was inciting pyro-antics among the show's fans, and the skit was eventually retired because of this controversy.

But the resultant publicity raised Jim Carrey's public profile. He did an HBO cable TV special and captured his first starring role in the movie *Ace Ventura: Pet Detective.* Released in February 1994 by Warner Bros., the madcap and sometimes very crude film comedy went on to gross more than $100 million, on only a $12 million budget.

Carrey's next effort, *The Mask,* came out in July of that same year and grossed $320 million worldwide on a $20 million budget.

And in December of 1994, New Line Cinema's *Dumb & Dumber,* teaming Carrey with actor Jeff Daniels and the brothers Farrelly (writer Bobby and co-writer/director Peter) became his third huge screen hit of the year, grossing $127 million.

Suddenly, dumb humor—the Three Stooges pie-in-the-face, Jerry Lewis falling-down-the-stairs kind—was back in style.

And Adam—with a little help from his friends—was about to capitalize on the trend, big-time.

CHAPTER 6

back to school

"Billy Madison [1995] was the first [movie] that I really got to get

creatively involved in, so that will always be my baby."

ADAM SANDLER, 1994

NOT EVERYONE WITH MAJOR TALENT GETS to be a big Hollywood star. It's one of the harsh realities of life that, frequently, whether your dreams come true often has little or nothing to do with your array of skills. Sometimes it's a matter of luck, being in the right place at the correct time, the way everyone associated with the surprise summer 1999 film hit *The Blair Witch Project* was. Sometimes it's a question of persistence: You just have to try, try, try again until you get noticed—witness rhythm and blues crooner Michael Bolton, who went through a long struggle as rock 'n' roll singer Michael Bolotin (on his own and with a band called *Blackjack*) before achieving superstar status in the mid-1980s.

And sometimes "making it" is simply a question of who you know—and what they can do for you. Just ask Tim Herlihy.

Although Adam was being comedic in the clubs in Los Angeles and New York, his old college roommate was cracking the books in law school. When Adam joined *SNL,* Tim joined a law firm down on Wall Street. The two remained close—Herlihy contributed to Sandler's 1993 album, *They're All Gonna Laugh at You*—but they weren't working together consistently, the way they had in their days as NYU students.

Then, at Adam's urging, Tim received a two-week tryout on the *SNL* writing staff toward the end of the 1993–94 season. Herlihy arranged a leave of absence from his law firm and settled into an NBC network office at 30 Rockefeller Plaza.

He passed the audition with flying colors and was hired the next season as a full-time staff writer. Today, he is the show's producer.

The other thing that happened at about the same time as Herlihy's *SNL* tryout, however, was even more important for the future of both Tim and Adam. He and Adam sat down to co-author a screenplay. What they came up with was the first draft of *Billy Madison*—which Adam showed to his *Airheads* (1994) producer, Robert Simonds. Simonds passed the script on to Universal executive Hal Lieberman—who green-lighted the picture in April 1994.

Adam, however, was hardly done with helping his pals.

He brought Jack Giarraputo onto the new screen project as associate producer. And he strongly suggested the studio hire a relative unknown named Steven Kessler to direct the comedy.

Back in the late 1980s, when Adam was a struggling stand-up comedian scrounging for work, Kessler had been the first person to hire him for some commercial work the director was then doing. Sandler never forgot the favor, and, when the opportunity came, pushed Kessler forward for his next film entry. Besides, Kessler was fully qualified for the job, as his 1991 short film, *Birch Street Gym,* had been nominated for an Academy Award. To the surprise of many insiders, Universal agreed to Sandler's choice of directors.

Making the behind-the-scenes set his own was just the first clue as to how heavily involved Adam was to be in every aspect of his debut as a full-fledged motion picture star. In a way, he was following in the footsteps of *SNL* contemporary Mike Myers, who had done the same thing for 1992's *Wayne's World* and its sequel, which came out a year later. Unlike Myers, however, Adam had been intent on coming up with an original concept for his first motion picture. There had been talk over the years of an Operaman movie, but Sandler had always rejected the idea. "I wanted to play a character from a real movie script," he would later tell Kate Meyers of *Entertainment Weekly* in February 1995, "not trade off the *SNL* show."

Adam also wanted to maintain creative control on the project, to ensure that it was, in fact, targeted for his special audience— for the people who continued to keep *They're All Gonna Laugh at You* on *Billboard*'s Heatseekers chart and continued to help sell-out his stand-up appearances. Those fans were the MTV generation, for lack of a better term.

In the plot line devised by Sandler and Herlihy, the son of a soon-to-retire hotel magnate discovers his dad plans to leave the company in the control of one of his employees, rather than keep it in the family. The reason for this decision is that the father considers his only child incompetent. The young man makes a wager with his parent: He'll go back and finish high school. At which point, the father informs his offspring that the only reason he even graduated grade school was because the teachers were rewarded handsomely. Nonetheless, the hero agrees to complete all twelve grades of school in just six months. Dad takes the bet— and *Billy Madison* is off and running.

The script offered Adam a chance to draw on his own experiences at Webster Elementary, Hillside Junior High, and Central High School back in Manchester, New Hampshire—where he had not exactly lit up the halls with stellar academic achievements. The movie assignment, Adam admitted, would be the closest thing he'd come to playing himself oncamera so far. It meant a lot to him, as he told *Entertainment Weekly*'s Kate Meyers. "I want it to be as good as it could be," he declared. To ensure that it was, he and Herlihy worked overtime on the script, executing rewrite after rewrite.

"We'd argue for hours about whether someone says 'Come on in' or 'come on in and have a seat,'" co-scripter Tim Herlihy related in the same article. He and Adam incorporated in-jokes for Sandler's long-time fans (a demented cafeteria worker quoted lines from "Lunchlady Land"). They wrote in parts for their *SNL* buddies Chris Farley and Norm Macdonald (other cameos included appearances by former *SNL* writer Robert Smigel and actor Steve Buscemi). Above all, they made sure it was funny to themselves and to their friends.

"My goal," Adam explained to *Entertainment Weekly*, "was to make sure people my age would like the movie."

Shooting for *Billy Madison* took place over *SNL*'s 1994 summer hiatus, at locations in and around Vancouver, British Columbia, Canada—where a good many American pictures were shot because production costs were less than in Hollywood. Adam's costars included film and television veteran Darren McGavin (best known as TV's *The Night Stalker*) as Billy's father, Brian Madison; actress Bridgitte Wilson as Vicki Vaughan, the third-grade teacher with whom Adam's character falls in love; Josh Mostel as the school's principal; and Bradley Whitford as villainous Eric Gordon, who will take over the hotel chain if Billy loses his bet.

Relatively speaking, *Billy Madison* was a very economically made movie, with a no-frills cast. This was just how Adam wanted it. He'd been around enough film sets to know that major studios tended to stay very close to their bigger investments and micromanage. (And even without his recent movie experience, all the troubles *SNL* was having certainly pointed toward the same lesson with Sandler.) The last thing Adam wanted was constant phone calls from studio executives interrupting the flow of work.

But early in the film's production, those calls from studio executives started coming anyway. The reason? The suits had decided that Steven Kessler was not the right individual for *Billy Madison* after all. The director agreed to leave the shoot.

"The studio wanted a less stylized movie, more of me being a goof," said Sandler. "It was very sad, like breaking up with a girlfriend," Adam informed *Entertainment Weekly*'s Kate Meyers in early 1995.

To replace Kessler, the studio turned to Tamra Davis. She was perhaps best known for her work on the R-rated *CB4* (1993)—a rap version of *This Is Spinal Tap* (1984)—which costarred (among others) *SNL* players Chris Rock and Phil Hartman. Davis found herself immediately thrust into the middle of Adam's special world.

One of her biggest challenges came when it was time to lense the parties Billy throws to celebrate his graduation from each grade. The producers had chosen the famous Parkwood Estate and Gardens—a world-renowned estate in Oshawa, Ontario, Canada (about twenty miles outside Toronto) that once belonged to the McLaughlin family who founded General Motors of Canada—as the site for the onscreen festivities. In the context of the movie's narrative these parties happened every few weeks: In real life, the shots were all completed over the span of just a few days. The manicured lawns and elegant fountains were overrun with clowns, animals, circus performers, seals, dozens of children, and, of course, Adam. It was a veritable zoo of talent to coordinate and keep track of. Davis had her hands full, particularly given the fact that the fun often didn't stop when she called "cut." The youngsters—sometimes joined by Sandler—had a tendency to keep going.

Adam's workday didn't end when the last scene was shot. "He'd call me every night after dailies, and we'd talk about the movie for an hour," director Davis later told *Entertainment Weekly.*

The comedy wrapped its shoot in August 1994. It would take several months of post-production (that is, looping dialog, scoring, editing, and so on) before the completed footage would be ready to test screen.

In the meantime, it was back to New York for Adam, for yet another year of *Saturday Night Live.*

○   ○   ○

The broadcast season of 1994–95 was to be *Saturday Night Live*'s twentieth on the air. No one was more excited than Adam at the news that several *SNL* veterans—including Dan Aykroyd and Bill

Murray of the original Not Ready for Prime Time Players—had been invited back to host episodes of the series during its special commemorative season. "It's going to be surreal," Adam confided to Cindy Pearlman of *Entertainment Weekly* (July 29, 1994). "Bill Murray came by recently to talk. There's nothing better than when Bill says, 'Hey, that thing you did was funny.'"

Yet the lingering effects of the previous TV season—critical drubbings, slipping ratings, disillusioned, disaffected staff and cast—could still be palpably felt. "I would question the grip on reality of anyone in my position who wasn't depressed at certain points last season," said returning producer/head writer James Downey, who had been shouldered with much of the blame for *SNL*'s troubles the previous year. And still more change was in the air as the new season began.

This time, it was the *SNL* cast, not the writing staff, receiving the overhaul. Phil Hartman had resigned, as had Julia Sweeney and Adam's good friend Rob Schneider. Melanie Hutsell and Sarah Silverman were let go. Chris Elliott (from the David Letterman TV talk show) and Janeane Garofalo (fresh off critically acclaimed roles in *The Larry Sanders Show* and the 1994 Gen-X film *Reality Bites*) joined Adam and fellow returnees Ellen Cleghorne, Chris Farley, Michael McKean (who'd come aboard the program in mid-season the previous year), Tim Meadows, Mike Myers, Kevin Nealon, and David Spade as full cast members.

Other *SNL* changes included Kevin Nealon giving up his role as "Weekend Update" anchor to return to doing sketches. Norm Macdonald (who'd been elevated from featured player to full cast member) was chosen as his replacement. Al Franken and Jay Mohr were back as featured players, joined by newcomers Laura Kightlinger and Molly Shannon.

New cast member Garofalo, for one, felt the series needed fixing.

"I'm hoping things change," she declared in an October 2, 1994, interview with Jim Slotek of the *Toronto Sun*. "*Saturday Night Live,* the last two years, has been unwatchable. The tension there is painful the second you walk through the door."

Other newcomers disagreed.

"Nothing's worse than I thought it was going to be, and many things are a lot better," Michael McKean (who had played Lenny Kosnowski on TV's *Laverne & Shirley*) told Dave Walker of the *Arizona Republic* in September 1994. "I see everyone looking for stuff that's a little challenging. That's what *Saturday Night Live* became famous for, taking risks."

As for Adam, even after the success of his album, after the high of making his movie, he still regarded studio number 8-H as his real home.

"*SNL* is the most important thing to me right now," he stressed to *Boston Herald* writer Paul Sherman in July 1994. "I hear Eddie Murphy and the guys who left the show talk, and even though they're the largest movie stars, they always talk about how much fun it was and how much they miss it. . . . As long as I can do it, I'm going to do it."

SNL's twentieth season debuted on September 24, 1994, appropriately enough, with a show emceed by perennial host Steve Martin, and with musical guest Eric Clapton. Some critics were impressed. David Bianculli (*New York Daily News*) wrote "The writers need to develop better scripts, but there's a strong team here with which they can work." Others, however, were not enthused at all. The opening episode felt worse than being "smashed over the head with a hammer for ninety minutes" according to John Podhoretz (*New York Post*).

Michaels and most of the cast were surprised by the ferocity of the critics' fresh attacks. "I think it's crazy, the amount of slamming we take from the press," Adam declared in a February 10, 1995, piece published in the *Asheville* (North Carolina) *Citizen-Times*. He tried to focus on the show: During the year, his Operaman character returned, and Adam introduced a new member in his stable of "Weekend Update" commentators. Gil Graham (Adam in a horrendous orange-colored wig, thick glasses, and a torn shirt) is another loveable loser: a would-be hipster whose every attempt to get into the rock concerts he is supposed to review is thwarted by beatings, bad timing, and bad dates. (So clearly is Gil an Adam Sandler character that Norm Macdonald, thanking Gil after his first oncamera appearance, accidentally calls him "Adam.")

Sandler added to his list of impressions during the TV year as well, doing Steven Tyler, Tom Jones, and a member of *Boyz II Men*. He did a new song for Valentine's Day, and gave his annual inexpensive Halloween costume tips. In a skit he repeatedly cited as one of his favorites, he and Dana Carvey—who returned as part of the twentieth-anniversary celebration to host an episode (October 24, 1994)—played two pepper millers: the master (Carvey) and his apprentice (Sandler).

But the *SNL* viewership ratings continued to slide: The 1993–94 season had been down 11 percent from 1992–93. In its showcase twentieth year, *SNL*'s ratings slid yet another 20 percent.

No matter what they tried, the cast and crew couldn't seem to find their proper oncamera stride. In a review of the Dana Carvey–hosted installment, *Daily Variety* declared, "It's dismaying the show doesn't seem fresher." Sketch after sketch was written reacting to the program's continual bashing or commenting on

the show's long history. To open the season premiere, several of
the cast (including Adam) auditioned for Phil Hartman's old job
as the show's resident President Clinton impersonator: In the
Carvey-hosted outing, ex-President Bush made a cameo, threatening to stop watching if the skits got too long. On an entry
(December 17, 1994) hosted by boxer George Foreman, Tim
Meadows (as Bruce Banner) turned into the Incredible Hulk
(Foreman): Foreman-as-Hulk dragged the sketch's writers
onstage and berated them for the routine's length and repetitive
nature. In the same show, Sandler did a dead-on impersonation
of bandleader/lead guitarist G. E. Smith, often picked on by the
press for his own continuous mugging to the camera.

The year before, Adam's "The Thanksgiving Song" from the
They're All Gonna Laugh at You album had received significant
airplay on alternative (read: college) radio charts, thanks to a
performance on *SNL*. Lorne Michaels noted the song's popularity and urged Sandler to do something similar for Chanukah.

"I was walking down the street when I thought up the first
line," Adam later told writer Naomi Pfefferman of the *Jewish
Journal*. "It went, 'Paul Newman is half Jewish: Goldie Hawn is
half too. Put them together: what a fine-looking Jew!'"

Adam debuted "The Chanukah Song" in the December 3,
1994, episode hosted by Roseanne. It was one of the season's
few highlights.

SNL was no longer doing what Michael McKean had rightly
pointed out it was famous for—pushing the envelope. Earlier in
the year, on November 8, 1994, Michael O'Donoghue, one of
SNL's original writer/performers, the man who'd spoken the very
first lines in its very first skit ("I'd like to feed your fingertips to
the wolverines," he'd told John Belushi), a man who many felt

epitomized the edge the show's current incarnation lacked, died of a brain hemorrhage. He was fifty-four years old.

It was an omen of things to come.

In the midst of all the gloom and doom surrounding *Saturday Night Live* in late 1994, Adam finally received a piece of good news: *Billy Madison* was finished. And the film was testing through the roof, particularly with the thirty-five and under crowd. Universal Pictures was so high on the movie, in fact, that even before it opened they contracted Adam and Tim Herlihy to write another one for the studio.

"They have a nice feeling about *Billy,*" Adam told Jim Slotek of the *Toronto Sun* at the time.

The studio—quite possibly at Adam's urging—also came up with a unique marketing stunt to help promote *Billy Madison.* The week before it opened, Adam, with a considerable media contingent in tow, flew back to New Hampshire to revisit Manchester's Central High School.

His old nemesis, Vice Principal Isabel Pellerin, was waiting for him. "I was threatening to stencil your name on your chair in detention," she told Adam. "Now I realize you were just rehearsing."

He spent time with Vice Principal Michael Clemons, who was flattered to learn that Sandler had named one of the characters in *Billy Madison* after him—until he got a look at the film's Mr. Clemens (a scrawny old man who is the victim of a very crude practical joke).

As it developed, Universal's confidence in the screen comedy was not misplaced.

On Friday, February 10, 1995, *Billy Madison* debuted in 1,834 theaters nationwide. After the weekend box-office receipts were counted, it emerged as the number one movie in America, grossing close to $7 million, and beating out such major studio productions as Sharon Stone's western *The Quick and the Dead* and Brad Pitt's *Legends of the Fall* (admittedly in its seventh week of release).

At last, Adam had made the movie for which his audience had been waiting.

The critics, on the other hand, were not so easily pleased.

"One of the most execrable movies ever made," insisted *Time* magazine's Richard Schickel. "The equivalent of a contact lobotomy," judged the *Philadelphia Inquirer.* "Feels like a prolonged *SNL* sketch in search of a funny exit," complained the *Hollywood Reporter's* Michael Rechstaffen.

The nation's tastemakers didn't much care for Adam's performance, either. According to them, Sandler was "someone who can only safely be taken in small, non-toxic doses" (Barbara Shulgasser of the *San Francisco Herald-Examiner*), and certainly "no Jim Carrey" (Rechtstaffen of the *Hollywood Reporter*). Brian Lowery (*Variety*) judged, "Those unfamiliar with Sandler's antics may also begin to find him annoying sometime between the appearance of the Universal logo and the end of the opening credits."

What virtually all the critics missed, despite their attempts to pigeonhole the picture and Sandler as Jim Carrey wannabes, was that this screen comedy, for all the rough spots in its eighty-eight minutes, had at its core a character with heart. Unlike the airheaded, unlikable protagonists in so many of the other "teen comedies" (such as Pauly Shore's 1993 entry *Son-in-Law,* 1994's *D2: The Mighty Ducks,* 1995's *Jerky Boys*) being forced down America's throat at the time, *Billy Madison* was somebody audiences could root for at the same time they were laughing at him.

Another point in the movie's favor, as Rita Kempley of the *Washington Post* correctly pointed out, "There's a moral to this story." At the end of the PG-13-rated entry, Billy decides that rather than work in the family business, he, too, wants to become a teacher. There were other kind words in the press. Virtually everyone had good things to say about Steve Buscemi's cameo performance, and most praised Chris Farley's turn as the demented school bus driver. The *Boston Globe* was one of the few papers to publicly applaud Adam's latest screen work, particularly enjoying the grade-school vignettes: "Sandler . . . is a hoot when he's playing off, or buying into, whatever grade he is thrust into: He's a doofus, a wise-acre, and most always a better human specimen than his addled, pre-rehab self."

There was something of the little kid in Adam's reaction to *Billy Madison*'s initial release: He spent the weekend of its debut driving around to local shopping malls, anxious to find out if people were actually going to see his starring vehicle.

By Monday, though, he had other things to worry about.

○　　　○　　　○

A quote from Adam appeared in a brief news item in the February 11, 1995, issue of *TV Guide*.

"It's no fun being recognized on the streets of New York," Adam declared (according to the article), "and the first thing people say is, 'Do movies' cause your show ain't happening."

The headlines came a couple of days later.

"Sandler says 'Writing on *SNL* sucks,'" was the gist of what the mainstream press reported. And suddenly the media, who had spent the week before jumping on *Billy Madison*, were climbing all over Adam again.

Within a day, Adam denied making the harsh statement. "As one of the writers on *SNL*, I obviously don't think our work sucks," he told the *Hollywood Reporter* on February 14, 1995. Sandler claimed he was "completely misquoted." But, the damage was done.

It's hard not to trace Adam's ongoing present disillusionment with the print media to this particular period: the bashing *Billy Madison* received, the flap over his controversial *TV Guide* comments, and the audible "I told you so's" coming from critics when, as if to confirm their judgement, *Billy Madison* virtually disappeared from theaters six weeks after its release. Naysayers were happy to deem the film a flop regardless of the fact that the movie had grossed $25 million at the box office, generating—given the film's $10 million budget—the start of a healthy profit for Universal. These earnings would grow to include revenue from foreign distribution, pay and broadcast TV, and home video.

Meanwhile, on *SNL*, things were going from bad to worse.

In March 1995, NBC president Warren Littlefield fired another shot at Lorne Michaels, suggesting that the creator/executive producer was not living up to his promise to improve the show. Michaels, in turn, was hurt reportedly by the lack of support from his network bosses, and blamed them for using micromanagement.

The ferocity of the attacks puzzled the cast as well. "We get it, we understand, we get the message," David Spade told Alan Bash of *USA Today* (April 3, 1995). "Some sketches are long, the writing is a little soft, there's too many in the cast." The failures weren't for lack of effort on anyone's part: "We all try our hardest to come up with stuff that makes people laugh," Adam said in his talk with the *Asheville* (North Carolina) *Times*.

The year before, Michaels had called a closed-door meeting between cast and crew to encourage all to be more supportive of each other. Lorne had insisted on a more professional attitude from all, on- and offcamera. No backstage bickering, no "unnamed sources" going to the media and airing the show's internal disputes.

This season, however, there was no hiding the show's troubles, as the conflicts were out in the open. Newcomer Janeane Garofalo was one of the most outspoken in her dissatisfaction with the shape of *SNL*.

"I like Janeane," David Spade told reporter Bash. "But I do get kind of fed up with constantly hearing things [before] we see her, and she says, 'Sorry about that, I didn't really say that.' And then two days later, it's like another blistering thing."

One of those blistering things she said concerned Adam.

"I think [he's] got the high school market cornered," she told Jim Slotek of the *Toronto Sun*. "All the boys who love to fart in class love Adam Sandler."

Janeane left the cast in mid-season, ostensibly on a "leave of absence." (This, however, wouldn't be the last time Garofalo would damn Adam with faint praise.)

The atmosphere at *SNL* continued to deteriorate. It reached a low point when, a few episodes before season's end, Mike Myers—probably the biggest remaining name in the cast—departed as well. Prophetically enough, on the year's last show, broadcast on May 13, 1995, in virtually the last sketch aired, Adam and Chris Farley were eaten by a polar bear.

It was good preparation for what was to come.

CHAPTER 7

starting over

"SNL was the best five years of my life . . . but I feel I've done all

I can do there and it's time to try other things."

ADAM SANDLER, JULY 1995

THIS WAS NOT HOW THE STORY was supposed to end.

Adam wanted to stay with *Saturday Night Live.* Right up until the day he walked out the door of the NBC network studio in midtown Manhattan, he told everyone who would listen that he had no intention of leaving the famed TV show. Talking with host Conan O'Brien on the June 10, 1995, edition of NBC-TV's *Late Night,* he referenced two new characters he was working on for the 1995–96 *SNL* season—the "Laugh-to-Dog Guy" (when he laughs, he becomes a dog), and the "crazy procrastinator behind the chair" man. Whether either of those concepts would have become full-fledged sketches on *SNL* will never be known.

On July 6, 1995, in a simple statement released to the media, Sandler declared that he had asked for, and received permission, to be let out of his *SNL* contract, which still had a year to run. What happened to change his mind?

No doubt there were several factors in Adam's decision (the furor from his comments the previous season, the internal turmoil, constant carping from NBC executives about cast members "phoning in" their performances), but in retrospect, one in particular stands out.

It was no secret that NBC executives—and to a certain extent, *SNL*'s production staff—were not happy about the show being perceived as what "the performers did in between movies." In the summer of 1995, word got out that upper management was about to impose significant new restrictions on *SNL*'s cast: No one would be released from their obligations to the weekly TV show to shoot a movie during the broadcast season, no matter how advantageous a filming schedule could be arranged.

Once he heard of those new work restrictions, Adam's return to New York City's 30 Rockefeller Plaza and the NBC network was a practical impossibility. He certainly didn't want what happened to Chris Farley (who, because of his commitment to *SNL*, lost the lead role—and a $5 million payday—for 1995's *The Cable Guy* to Jim Carrey) to befall him.

For much the same reasons, one suspects, Chris Farley followed Adam out the *SNL* door a week later.

The rest of the cast was not far behind. In all, thirteen of the show's seventeen performers left in mid-1995. Of the full cast members only Norm Macdonald and David Spade returned for *SNL*'s twenty-first season in the fall of 1995.

In the least surprising development of all, *SNL* producer/head writer Jim Downey was out. NBC network's top exec Don Ohlmeyer declared that Downey's head writer position would not be filled. (In mid-July of 1995, Ohlmeyer suggested to Jane Hall of the *Los Angeles Times* that having everything go through one writer "may have led to homogeneity.") The writing staff would undergo wholesale changes, ultimately ending with nine new members. (Tim Herlihy was one of the only returnees to that department.) Longtime director Dave Wilson was let go, as was G. E. Smith, who'd been *SNL*'s bandleader since 1986.

In the September 19, 1999, issue of the *New York Times*, *Saturday Night Live*'s creator/executive producer, Lorne Michaels, revealed to reporter Bill Carter that much of the personnel turnover had been ordered by Ohlmeyer and his NBC cohorts.

"Don Ohlmeyer wanted me to . . . dynamite the whole thing and start over again. . . . I was told to get rid of people." One of those people, according to Michaels, was Adam, who still had two years remaining on his contract with the show. NBC executives simply didn't find Sandler's humor to their taste—an opinion they were none too shy about expressing.

Ultimately, whether or not Adam's departure from *SNL* was voluntary is beside the point. Given the restrictions on his movie career cited above, the show's continued ratings slide, and the pressure on Michaels generated by NBC, his departure was inevitable.

In providing commentary on what essentially was the end of a TV era, Ohlmeyer contended that the *SNL* of the previous few years hadn't provided any breakout performers "like Dana Carvey or Billy Crystal."

Neither, one is forced to add, has the *SNL* of the years since 1995's massive turnover. In fact, the show remains much as before: wildly uneven, albeit with a fresh roster of oncamera personalities. Those performers (such as Will Ferrell, Chris Kattan, Ana Gasteyer, Darrell Hammond, and Jim Breuer), while undeniably talented, have yet to create a single character that has really captured the country's imagination.

Adam Sandler, meanwhile, has created several on the big screen: Billy Madison, Robbie Hart, Bobby Boucher, Sonny Koufax . . .

Although Adam Sandler's formal association with *Saturday Night Live* was over, in the public's mind—and certainly, among themselves—he and his former cast mates were still close, especially when it came to comparing the success of their respective movie careers. Sandler joked about the competition they all felt with writer Mal Vincent of the (Norfolk) *Virginian-Pilot* back in the summer of 1994.

"All the guys sit around during rehearsals on *Saturday Night Live* and we talk about who's going to break through, and I'm thinking, *I know I'm going to make more money than these guys, but will that affect our friendship?*"

A year later, in July of 1995, surveying the movie box-office track records of Adam and his *SNL* contemporaries, most people would not have picked Sandler as the group's breakout movie star.

Chris Farley, whose outsized persona had made him the most visible of the ex-*SNL* crowd, whose 1995 film *Tommy Boy* (which had paired him with David Spade in a script written by

SNL writers Bonnie and Terry Turner) had grossed more than $30 million and prompted the $5 million offer for Farley to star in *The Cable Guy*, was gathering most of the media attention.

Another more likely star-in-the-making than Adam was Mike Myers. Despite the relative failure of 1993's *So I Married an Axe Murderer* (total gross: $12 million) and *Wayne's World 2* (which took in barely $50 million at the box office, compared to the $170 million the first *Wayne's World* had gathered), he was still one of the most recognizable and popular of the *SNL* crowd with filmgoers.

Among the others one would more likely have chosen was Rob Schneider. Although he had yet to receive top billing in any feature film, Schneider had actually assembled the most varied resume of all the 1990s *SNL* alumni, with roles in *Necessary Roughness* (1991), *Home Alone 2: Lost in New York* (1992), *The Beverly Hillbillie*s (1993), the Sylvester Stallone/Wesley Snipes action entry, *Demolition Man* (1993), and so on.

In fact, right after Sandler's departure from *SNL*, Adam received a message on his answering machine from Rob Schneider, which said in part: "Feel that wind? That was the sound of me going by you." The message was prompted by the rave notices Schneider was receiving for his work ("a movie-stealing performance," according to Barry Koltnow of the *Phoenix* (Arizona) *Gazette*) in 1995's *Judge Dredd*, starring opposite Sly Stallone.

Schneider's career star was certainly on the rise. And to many observers, Adam's seemed as clearly on the wane. He was through at *SNL*. *Billy Madison*'s relatively modest box-office success at the beginning of 1995 was a memory. To add to all this, his comedy album *They're All Gonna Laugh at You* was, at last, slipping down the Heatseekers chart.

"Find a day job, quick," writer Walt Belcher of the *Tampa* (Florida) *Tribune* advised Sandler. Other members of the press concurred.

Things weren't looking good professionally for Adam as the summer of 1995 began.

And then they got worse.

◯   ◯   ◯

During his time with *SNL*, Adam virtually lived at his Manhattan office for those twenty-odd weeks a year when the show broadcast live. And even though Sandler had a million other things going on in his life as well (stand-up appearances, comedy albums, and so on), there were times when he was still able to step back from the pressure cooker and relax.

The demands of being a film star, though, were something else again.

It wasn't just the time he spent on the set. It was the many hours he devoted to every aspect of production. Making a modern motion picture can be split into three distinct phases: pre-production (casting characters, choosing locations, hiring crew, and so on), shooting, and post-production (editing, inserting special effects, dubbing dialog, scoring music, and so on). Each part can take anywhere from weeks to months, depending on the availability of personnel and studio facilities and the type of movie being made (*Jurassic Park* versus, for example, *Billy Madison*).

Adam wanted to have a say in every decision related to his films. It was part of the reason he'd brought in a production team with whom he was very comfortable. His intention was not to dictate his desires and watch them carried out (no one gets far in any business with that kind of behavior), but to have people around him who were simpatico to his taste and style.

Being that involved, though, took up a lot of Adam's time and energy, leaving him with little of either to spend in other areas of his life. Like his relationships with friends, family . . . and longtime girlfriend Margaret Ruden.

In a 1994 question and answer session with performer Ben Stiller for *Interview* magazine, Adam had declared that "doing *Saturday Night Live* definitely affects my relationship with my girlfriend and with my family, because you feel so much pressure to do well that night [but] everyone's grown to accept that and so they give me my space at the show."

Giving Sandler his space at the show was one thing. But as he spent more and more time on his film career, what little he and Margaret Ruden had together was being eaten away. To his credit, Adam, now approaching age thirty, recognized what was happening. As he admitted to Stiller in the *Interview* piece, however, he was afraid to pass up his chance at achieving his career dreams.

"You never know when this s*** is going to be taken away from us. That's why right now I'm working as hard as I can to make sure I get the best possible run I can get."

Adam and Margaret (according to some reports) had actually planned a big wedding for September 1995, to be held at the plush Ritz-Carlton in Laguna Niguel, California. Invitations had gone out, and RSVPs were coming back in when the two called off first the ceremony, and then, their relationship.

Some reports had Adam making the decision, although others attributed the breakup to Margaret. The truth probably lay somewhere in between. Despite the genuine affection between the two of them, each recognized that their lives were heading in far different directions. As a rising executive in the cosmetics industry, Margaret had a full life in New York City. Adam's energies were focused on the film industry, and this was centered in Los Angeles.

None of these rationales, however, made the split any easier.

Soon enough, the press would begin to link Adam romantically with other celebrities, including Chrissy Hynde of the rock band the Pretenders, and most prominently, young actress Alicia Silverstone, best known for her role in the screen comedy *Clueless* (1995) and for appearing in a half-dozen Aerosmith music videos.

In the summer of 1995, however, Adam's focus was not on his love life. It was on his profession . . . and, curiously enough, his golf game.

○   ○   ○

For his second major starring role in the movies, Adam, with his co-writer Tim Herlihy, again drew on Sandler's youth in Manchester, New Hampshire, for story-line inspiration. More specifically, they focused on one of Adam's childhood buddies, a young man named Kyle who eventually would play pro hockey in Norway. It was how Kyle applied his hockey skills to another sport, however, that provided the screenplay's basic premise.

As Sandler later recalled, one day his father Stanley (himself an excellent golfer) had invited the boys along to play. To everyone's surprise, Kyle beat the elder Sandler. Adam told writer Karen Hershenson of the *Knight-Ridder* syndicate in February 1996: "He didn't really know how to play, he just smacked the ball real far."

To this rather unique skill, co-writers Adam and Tim added the unique Sandler touch. As opposed to the real-life Kyle, "Happy Gilmore"—the name the two came up with for their leading character—was simply not a very good hockey player. The comedy opens with Happy having failed (for the tenth consecutive year) to make his local hockey squad. Not only that, but his girlfriend has dumped him, and—most importantly—his grandmother's home, the house where she raised him after his father's accidental death, has just been repossessed by the Internal Revenue Service. Soon thereafter, Happy's grandmom is sent to a nursing home. Meanwhile, the hapless hero learns he has six months to come up with $270,000, or grandma's house will be auctioned off by the government.

It is at this juncture that (fortuitously enough) Happy discovers he has the ability to drive a golf ball considerably farther than anyone who's ever played the game. He joins the pro tour, where his unique swing and National Hockey League–inspired behavior make him the tour's leading spectator attraction. Eventually, Happy wins enough money to buy back his grandmother's house, and, in the process, he even finds a new love.

"I've known a lot of guys like Happy," Adam enthused to the *Boston Globe* in 1996. "There's one at every construction site. One in every electrical contracting business. He's determined. He's nice to his girlfriend and his grandma. He's a hero. He's a leading man. And the best part is, he gets to be one without being soft and sweet."

For the new project (again, being backed by Universal), Robert Simonds and Jack Giarraputo were back on the production team, joined by talent managers/producers Bernie Brillstein and Brad Grey, as well as by Adam's new manager, Sandy Wernick. Locations were set—most of the picture would again be shot in more economical Canada, with additional filming to be done at golf links in San Francisco and Fort Lauderdale, Florida.

In assembling the crew and cast, Simonds brought along Dennis Dugan (who'd helmed the first *Problem Child* for him) as director. In addition, Adam's NYU buddy Allen Covert joined the team, cast as Happy's caddy, Otto. The film's costars included Julie Bowen as the hero's love interest, tour publicity director Virginia Venit; Carl Weathers (best known for his recurring role as Apollo Creed in the first three *Rocky* features, and as the Chief of Police in the last two years, 1993–94, of the long-running TV police drama *In the Heat of the Night*) as Happy's golfing tutor, club pro Chubbs Peterson; and Christopher MacDonald (Geena Davis's husband in 1991's *Thelma & Louise*) as Happy's nemesis, Shooter McGavin.

The script (which benefited from some uncredited touching-up by another of Adam's old NYU pals, screenwriter Judd Apatow, as well as Dean Lorey) also contained a number of terrific supporting roles. One in particular made everyone sit up and take notice: long-time game-show (*The Price Is Right*) host Bob Barker played himself, taking on Happy in a knock-down, drag-out fight during the plot's celebrity pro-amateur golf tournament.

As veteran performer Barker later told talk-show host Larry King, it was Adam, who had watched *The Price Is Right* while growing up, who suggested Bob for the role once the part was written. In a February 13, 1996, interview with *USA Today* Barker revealed that once he saw the script and realized "I get to beat someone up and win," he decided the screen assignment was for him.

What no one appreciated at the time was that Barker, now in his seventies, had been studying karate for close to twenty years, and that his teachers included the illustrious black belter/movie star Chuck Norris.

Other celebrities who played themselves in the new film included golfer Lee Trevino ("every time Happy is doing something unconventional, we pan over to Lee shaking his head," Adam told Ruthe Stein of the *San Francisco Chronicle* in February 1996) and sports announcer Verne Lundquist. Kevin Nealon and Bob Smigel from *SNL* had parts in the movie, as did Adam's friend Ben Stiller. Ben made an uncredited appearance as a nursing home orderly. Director Dennis Dugan himself put in a brief appearance as the director of the golfing tour .

Even as *Happy Gilmore* was preparing to begin principal photography in July of 1995, Adam came to terms with Universal Pictures on a deal for his next movie, *Bulletproof* (1996). That project—an action-comedy—would mark a departure for Sandler. Not only was it a new screen genre for him to tackle, but, for the first time, Adam would share lead billing on a film.

The whole thing was actually his idea.

"I was the initiator," Adam would later tell writer Kristin Brannigan of the (Los Angeles) *Valley Vantage,* in a piece that ran in September 1996. "I wanted to do a movie with Damon [Wayans]." The two comedians had met during the 1994–95 season of *SNL* when Damon, who was a cast member in 1986, returned to host an episode (April 8, 1995) of the show during its twentieth-anniversary celebration.

For *Bulletproof, Variety* reported, Adam would receive an advance of $2.5 million dollars. Shortly thereafter, high-profile director Ernest Dickerson—best known for his work as Spike Lee's cinematographer on that filmmaker's early movies and his own directorial debut, the urban drama *Juice* (1992)—signed on to direct *Bulletproof.*

Sandler's career—seemingly on the skids just a few short months before—was firmly back on track.

On August 11, 1995, during the middle of young America's school vacation, the home video for *Billy Madison* was released. The movie rocketed to the top of the video rental charts, eventually earning close to $30 million from those receipts (a figure that actually surpassed its total box-office take.) Colleges across the country began having "Billy Madison" nights: Doubting industry observers began to have second thoughts about the size and strength of Adam Sandler's audience.

Adam himself was surprised by the renewed popularity of his first big league starring turn. "I'm always running into people who say, 'My kid's seen your video eighteeen times. . . . He won't return it," Sandler told writer Jennifer Weiner of the *Knight-Ridder* news service in early 1996.

Other studios now cast a covetous eye on Sandler and his creative team: New Line Cinema, who'd lost out to Universal in the bidding for *Bulletproof,* was foremost among them. Its studio president, Michael De Luca, convinced that Adam Sandler was the next big screen breakout comedy star, wanted the actor's next project to be for New Line.

De Luca and Adam's other studio suitors, however, would have to wait. Because right after *Happy Gilmore* finished shooting, Adam began preparation for his second comedy CD.

○   ○   ○

"What I love about Adam is that he rolls up his sleeves and works." That's producer Brooks Arthur talking, in an interview that later appeared on Warner Bros. Records official Adam Sandler Web site. Arthur repeated his role as Adam's "recording studio director" for the comic's second album, *What the Hell Happened to Me?* (1996).

"He's got some ideas, and I help him edit them before we record. We do lots of takes, and then we spend hours editing—sculpting—those takes into one."

"We" on the album's comedy tracks included college friends Judd Apatow, Allen Covert, Frank Coraci, and Tim Herlihy, as well as *SNL*'ers Ellen Cleghorne and Kevin Nealon. For the record's musical numbers, Adam and Brooks hired the cream of Los Angeles's studio musicians, including guitarist Waddy Wachtel (who'd worked with Keith Richards and Linda Ronstadt, among others), drummer Jim Keltner, bassist Bob Glaub, and multi-instrumentalist Teddy Castellucci, who would later became a key member of Sandler's film production team.

What the Hell Happened to Me? contained twenty tracks: seven songs (most significantly, a live version of "The Chanukah Song") and thirteen comedy sketches. The skits featured a mixture of Sandler characters, some new, some taken from his stand-up routines. In a February 1999 *Playboy* magazine interview, the comic/actor discussed the genesis of one of those new characters: "The Goat."

"When I first came to Los Angeles I used to drive past a goat in Van Nuys [a city located in the San Fernando Valley]. Every day this goat is standing in a pickup. You start to wonder—what's his story? So one night my buddies and I were driving to a Beastie Boys concert. We pass the goat and I start doing his voice: 'I'm stuck in this truck.' I decided the goat was from Europe. He gets beaten by the old man who brought him here, but the goat never gives up. He loves flowers . . . "

Although Adam had "The Goat" completely worked out in his mind before he entered the studio, other sketches were less defined: "The Hypnotist," for one, which Sandler performed with Kevin Nealon.

"We set up two separate mikes and did 'The Hypnotist' half a dozen times, improvising as we went," Brooks Arthur explained. "Then we took those takes into the editing room. We had our script supervisor type [them] out . . . then we'd listen to them and select what we wanted. Afterward, we added sound effects. It was like [working on] a film."

The album was finished in the fall of 1995. As the holidays approached, Warner Bros. Records released a radio-only version of "The Chanukah Song" to stations throughout the United States. They expected it would get modest airplay and perhaps generate a little anticipation for the pending CD release.

What happened next took everyone by surprise.

Driven by listener demand nationwide, "The Chanukah Song" shot into *Billboard*'s Hot #100 airplay chart, eventually peaking at #10. New York's leading Top 40 radio station, Z-100, received more than 20,000 requests weekly for the number. "We had to disregard every rule we'd ever set up for holiday songs and play it as often as we'd play Pearl Jam and Alanis Morissette," program director Steve Kingston told *Time* magazine in January 1996.

Adam Sandler had a hit song. And it couldn't have come at a better time—just a few weeks before the virtually simultaneous release of his CD *What the Hell Happened to Me?* and his new film *Happy Gilmore,* set to debut within a week of each other in February 1996.

Adam-mania was about to ignite, big-time.

○   ○   ○

Just before President's Day weekend in 1996, Universal kicked the publicity machine into high gear for *Happy Gilmore.* Adam and Bob Barker—whose onscreen fight the company correctly judged would draw significant media attention—did a series of interviews with the press, including one with Arlene Vigoda of *USA Today.*

"As I go on in my film career as an action hero, I will always remember the start that young Adam gave me," Barker joked. For his part, Sandler declared (with tongue firmly in cheek), "In real life, I know I could take Bob."

The PG-13–rated *Happy Gilmore* opened on February 16, 1996, in 2,022 theaters in the United States and Canada. The ninety-two-minute feature grossed $10.11 million its opening weekend, finishing behind the John Travolta/Christian Slater action entry, *Broken Arrow,* at $14.9 million and *Muppet Treasure Island,* which took in a scant $828 more than *Happy Gilmore.* (Adam would later tell TV talk-show host Jay Leno he felt guilty about taking box-office away from the Muppets because "Kermit the frog taught me the alphabet.")

The reviewers were kinder to *Happy* than they'd been to *Billy Madison.* Michael Rechtstaffen of the *Hollywood Reporter,* who'd savaged Sandler's first star turn a year earlier, declared Adam's second film "amicable entertainment . . . a funny golf film worthy of comparison with *Caddyshack.*" Rechtstaffen went on to praise cast and crew alike, particularly director Dennis Dugan's "nicely restrained comic touch." Los Angeles's *Entertainment Today* labeled the film "absolutely hilarious—stupid, but hilarious." *USA Today,* in giving the film three out of four stars, singled out Bob Barker's screen performance for praise.

Adam himself received good notices. The *Washington Post* judged his new screen work "genial and surprisingly self-contained. . . . He wisely abandons the whining boy routine, replacing it with a mischievous, good-natured and often endearing persona." "Sandler has a brash, funky charm," concurred the *San Francisco Chronicle*.

There were detractors, of course. *Variety*'s Brian Lowery charted, "Added together there are about three minutes of funny material in 'Happy Gilmore.' . . . Gauging the level of humor, 'Happy' makes the last major comedy set in the staid world of golf, 'Caddyshack,' look like 'Masterpiece Theatre.'" Roger Ebert, writing for the *Chicago Sun-Times*, gave the big-screen farce only half a star (out of four), while *US* magazine called *Happy Gilmore* "a one-joke *Caddyshack* for the blitzed and jaded." "Sandler's appeal remains a mystery," insisted *People*. "He is too sluggish and inexpressive a screen personality for his antics to convey kinetic excitement," decided Stephen Holden (*New York Times*). "Back to stand-up, Sandler," advised the *San Francisco Examiner*.

The critics, of course, did not buy tickets at the box office. The public did, and Adam's public loved his latest cinematic nonsensical excursion. With a budget of $12 million, *Happy Gilmore* was one of the most successful movies of 1996, grossing close to $39 million at the box office (and later, an additional $47 million on its video release).

At the Tenth Annual Nickelodeon Kids Choice Awards, the PG-13-rated *Happy Gilmore* was nominated for Best Picture. In addition, Adam and Bob Barker received an MTV Movie Award nomination for Best Fight.

The week after *Happy* opened, Adam's second comedy album, *What the Hell Happened to Me?* was released. It shot right up *Billboard*'s Hot #100 album charts, quickly landing in the top twenty-five.

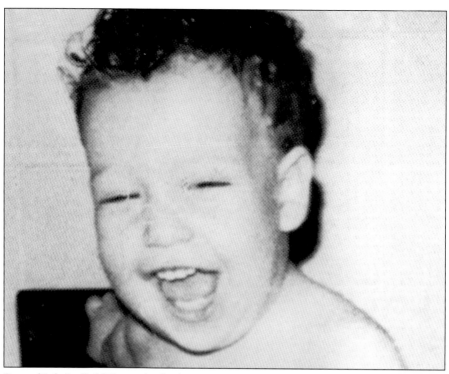

Stan and Judy Sandler's kid, mugging for the camera. (COURTESY OF SETH POPPEL YEARBOOK ARCHIVES)

Adam's 1984 graduation picture, Manchester Central High School in New Hampshire. (COURTESY OF SETH POPPEL YEARBOOK ARCHIVES)

Adam Sandler, would-be ladies' man. (COURTESY OF SETH POPPEL YEARBOOK ARCHIVES)

Manchester Central High's class clown(s). (COURTESY OF SETH POPPEL YEARBOOK ARCHIVES)

Adam and his *Saturday Night Live* cast members (1992). (COURTESY OF AP/WIDE WORLD PHOTOS)

Adam and fellow *Saturday Night Live* alumnus Jon Lovitz. (COURTESY OF LIAISON AGENCY)

Adam receives the 1999 Kids' Choice Award for "Favorite Movie Actor." (COURTESY OF ARCHIVE PHOTOS)

Adam takes it on the chin from his *Happy Gilmore* costar, Bob Barker, after their win for "Best Fight" at the 1996 MTV Movie Awards. (COURTESY OF ARCHIVE PHOTOS)

Adam with Cole and Dylan Sprouse, his *Big Daddy* (1999) costars, at the New York City premiere. (COURTESY OF LIAISON AGENCY)

The winner! Adam at the 1999 MTV Movie Awards with his trophy for "Best Comedic Performance" for *The Waterboy*. (COURTESY OF ARCHIVE PHOTOS)

Actress Drew Barrymore and Adam cut the cake for photographers a few days before the opening of *The Wedding Singer* (1998). (COURTESY OF ARCHIVE PHOTOS)

Adam plays it cool at a New York City premiere in 1998. (COURTESY OF LIAISON AGENCY)

"An infinite improvement over his first sad and unfunny record. . . . Sandler seems to be evolving out of juvenilia," decided *Cinemania Music Reviews*. Richard Zoglin, writing for *Time,* judged, "[Sandler] reveals some unforeseen talent on his new album . . . the best of his dry, absurdist bits . . . have more body and feeling for character than anything *SNL* offers these days."

Warner Bros. also released a video from the album to help promote the record to Adam's MTV audience. "Steve Polychronopolous" made its exclusive debut February 15, 1996, on the cable television channel Comedy Central.

"Steve Polychronopoulos is the kind of guy we all know," Sandler explained to *PR Newswire*. "He's a big stupid jerk, who drinks all of your beer, eats the last slice of pizza, spits when he talks, always needs a ride, and swears in front of your mother."

In the video, besides Adam playing Steve, there also appeared Bobcat Goldthwait, Garry Shandling, and *SNL*-ers past and present, including Tim Meadows, Rob Schneider, Chris Farley, David Spade, Norm Macdonald, and Colin Quinn.

Adam's mounting show business success made him one of those stars who people watched closely. *US* magazine chatted with him about his currently favorite restaurant (*Hugo's* in West Hollywood); *People* reported his dating habits (most notably, his relationship with actress Alicia Silverstone); and the national media noted how "The Chanukah Song" had inspired other stars to "come out" and proclaim their Jewish heritage.

Even with the media spotlight focused firmly on him, however, the most significant Adam Sandler–related news item of 1996 slipped by virtually unnoticed.

CHAPTER 8

different strokes

"As a writer, you want to come up with stuff you haven't done . . .

stuff you feel comfortable with and feel driven to do."

ADAM SANDLER, 1996

O N FEBRUARY 27, 1996, NEW LINE CINEMA'S president Michael De Luca finally snagged his man.

That was the day *Daily Variety*'s "News" column reported that Adam Sandler would be doing his next movie for New Line: The picture was to be titled *The Wedding Band*. Reporter Dan Cox described it as "a romantic comedy about a man whose love life is a complete disaster but whose job is to sing at the most romantic settings in the world as he hops from wedding to wedding."

You could almost hear the sound of the critics sharpening their knives at the announcement. Adam Sandler? In a romantic comedy? What was worse, in the eyes of many, was the actor's announced salary. Twenty-nine-year-old Sandler was to receive a whopping $5 million fee for his debut entry within a screen genre for which he had absolutely no experience. The deal was also reported as "pay-or-play," which meant that whether or not the film got made, New Line would have to put forth Sandler's entire film salary (generally speaking, studio deals defer a significant percentage of the star's announced fee until the movie is actually released).

The previous November, Chris Farley had received $6 million to do *Beverly Hills Ninja* (1997). The year 1995 had also seen Jim Carrey become Hollywood's first $20 million–man with the wages he'd received to take over Farley's part in *The Cable Guy* (1996). These astronomical salaries—and the relatively young stars who were getting them—set off a new round in the continuing debate on the popularity of "low-brow" comedy in America.

"You wonder when it's going to bottom out," director Barry Levinson, who'd worked briefly as a stand-up comedian himself, told writer Lawrence Christon of *Daily Variety* in February 1996. Levinson's humor-tinged films, such as *Diner* (1982) and *Tin Men* (1987), were the antithesis of the kinds of movies that actors such as Sandler, Carrey, Farley, and so forth were getting rich on: That is, Levinson's movies were thoughtfully plotted, meticulously crafted comedies whose humor arose from ordinary people trapped in extraordinary situations.

In other words, no bodily function jokes, as found frequently in the "new-breed" comedies of present-day Hollywood.

"Doesn't anyone wonder whether we'll be the poorer for all this [trend]?" asked veteran comedian/political satirist Mort Sahl in the same article.

While some of the old guard in Hollywood complained, others cashed in. For example, Jack Lemmon, who'd won Academy

Awards for his acting in *Mister Roberts* (1955) and *Save the Tiger* (1973), received the biggest salary of his career in March 1996: $5 million for agreeing to appear with his old *Odd Couple* (1968) costar Walter Matthau in a comedy to be called *Out to Sea* (1997). Even as he was signing the picture's contract, it's safe to say that Lemmon, now seventysomething, knew his work in that entry would not in any way contribute to the art of cinema. Why do it?

"I'm making nice money," the enduring actor told the *San Diego Union-Tribune* in March 1996.

No articles appeared bemoaning Lemmon's price tag for *Out to Sea*. Perhaps industry observers felt he deserved the "big bucks" after so many years in the business, as opposed to "upstarts" such as Sandler and Carrey.

Everyone seems to have missed the real point.

Studios do not do deals on which they don't expect to make money—a lot of money. They are willing to give actors such as Adam, Jim Carrey, Chris Farley, Pauly Shore, and David Spade millions of dollars because their presence in a film is as close to a safe bet as one can get in Hollywood. That is, a bet that the star's fans will happily plunk down $7.50 to see their hero on the big screen.

Studio executive Michael De Luca had seen the video rental numbers for Sandler's *Billy Madison* (1995) and the sales figures for the comic's CD *They're All Gonna Laugh at You*. He'd probably heard "The Chanukah Song" more than once on his car radio. It's certain he'd seen the box-office statistics for *Happy Gilmore* (1996). By guaranteeing Adam $5 million, De Luca and New Line Cinema were affirming their belief that Sandler's audience would show up in equal force for the upcoming *The Wedding Band*.

Actually, they were hoping for a bit more.

"This is the film that is going to expand Adam's box-office draw," Mitch Goldman, the studio's president of marketing and distribution, told *Variety*'s Adam Goldworm just prior to the finished movie's release in February 1998. "This is not just a niche film targeted only at college and high school kids. This is a romantic comedy for everyone."

Adam, for his part, didn't use words such as "demographics" or "box-office potential." He wasn't obsessed visibly with where his salary ranked him on Hollywood's latest hot list. He left the management of his money to his brother and father, with the exception of the fifty thousand or so dollars he had just used to buy his dad a Jaguar (one suspects he was similarly generous with other family members).

Sandler made his career choices, as he told writer Neal Justin of the *Minneapolis* (Minnesota) *Star-Tribune* in June 1996, on a far more intuitive basis: "I want to do something that makes me laugh, and I hope makes someone else laugh."

His intuition, however, was about to be proven wrong.

After leaving *SNL* in mid-1995, Adam became, for all intents and purposes, a full-time resident of Los Angeles (even though he still maintained an apartment in Manhattan). The adjustment was a difficult one, as he joked with TV talk-show host Jay Leno: The hardest thing was getting used to spending so much time in his car.

Still, living right near Hollywood had its advantages, one of them being that he didn't have far to travel when *Bulletproof* started shooting on March 20, 1996, in Los Angeles. The production team was largely composed of familiar faces: Adam's manager Sandy Wernick (helped out by Brad Grey and Bernie Brillstein) executive produced, Robert Simonds was producer, Jack Giarraputo and Ira Shuman co-producers, and Janine Sherman was the associate producer.

The story (also set in L.A.) follows the adventures of two con men—best friends Archie Moses (Adam) and Rock Keats (Damon Wayans). As the narrative begins, Archie introduces Rock to his boss, Frank Colton (James Caan, best known for his Oscar-nominated role as Sonny Corleone in 1972's *The Godfather*), a used car salesman who also happens to be the area's biggest drug dealer. What Archie doesn't realize is that Rock is actually an undercover policeman, who has been assigned to take down Colton's operation. Rock, who's been deceiving his supposed best friend for months while he worms his way into Archie's confidence, feels tremendous guilt at betraying his pal and wants to be the one to arrest him. The bust goes sour, however: And in the ensuing gunfight, Archie, furious at Rock for his betrayal, accidentally shoots and wounds his pal.

Moses soon realizes he's in a terrible jam: Not only has he shot a cop, but drug czar Colton wants to kill him too, convinced that he's betrayed the operation. Archie decides to turns himself in, and agrees to reveal the details of Colton's operation to the authorities under one condition: Rock (now recovered from his injury) must be the one who takes him on.

Keats agrees to the terms and heads south to rendezvous with Archie, when they're ambushed by Colton's thugs, who track them across the Southwest before the movie's final climax back in the City of Angels.

The rest of the cast included James Farentino as Rock's boss, Captain Jensen, and Kristen Wilson as Wayans's love interest/ physical therapist.

This, to put it mildly, was a different kind of Adam Sandler film. (In actuality, *Bulletproof* was also a racially inverted variation of 1982's *48 Hours,* which had starred Nick Nolte as the harassed law enforcer who uses convicted Eddie Murphy to help trap a crook.)

Within *Bulletproof,* there were no *SNL* guest stars, no celebrity cameos, and—with the exception of co-producer Giarraputo and actor Allen Covert, who made a brief appearance as one of Wayans's fellow detectives—no roles (on- or offcamera) for Sandler's New York University posse.

What moviegoers did get was a new facet of Sandler—Adam in his first big-screen dramatic appearance. Granted, there was a lot of comedy (much of which was improvised by Sandler and Wayans) in the finished eighty-five-minute film. The comedy, however, came out of their screen characters. The challenge Adam faced was similar to the one he'd tackled in *Airheads* back in 1994—to keep the story on track while making the audience laugh.

Staying focused oncamera wasn't just Sandler's task, of course. It was Wayans's—and to an even larger extent—the responsibility of director Ernest Dickerson.

"We needed someone who was going to get the shot, get the composition, help us stick to the story and pull us back from being funny when we needed to be serious," costar Damon told writer Kristin Brannigan of Los Angeles's *Valley Vantage* at the time of the film's release in September 1996. "That's what Ernest did [so] well."

Although the R-rated *Bulletproof* was designed to show audiences a new dimension of Adam Sandler, producer Robert Simonds was also hoping that the part of Rock Keats would be the movie role that would kick Wayans up to the next level of movie stardom.

"Damon's not just a comedian; he's a real actor, and a lot of people don't realize that yet," Simonds told journalist Barry Koltnow for the *Orange County* (California) *Register* (September 6, 1996). "But they'll realize it after this film. Damon is headed for superstardom."

Since he'd left *In Living Color* in 1992—the FOX-TV sketch comedy show his brother, Keenen Ivory Wayans, had created— Damon's box-office clout had diminished considerably. His last two releases, the superhero spoof *Blankman* (1994) and the army comedy *Major Payne* (1995) had taken in $8 and $29 million, respectively—not a good omen for the hoped-for longevity of his screen career.

Actually, Wayans's box-office high-water mark had come in 1991's *The Last Boy Scout* (in which he played second banana to action hero Bruce Willis), which grossed $88 million. Simonds and Universal Pictures executives (who had also released *Major Payne*) were no doubt hoping that the pairing of Sandler and Wayans would generate the same kind of box-office magic that Willis and Wayans in tandem had accomplished.

The story line of *Bulletproof* held a particular relevance for Wayans. He'd actually played the role of betrayed friend—in real life. "When I worked for American Express, I used to steal credit cards," he confessed to writer Brannigan of the *Valley Vantage*. "This undercover guy [pretended to be] my friend for about two months and then he turned around and busted me."

Adam brought no such baggage to his new screen assignment: He was looking to expand his range as an actor, work with Wayans, and meet James Caan.

"When I was a kid, my grandma used to say, 'You remind me of James Caan.' And I used to tell her, 'I'm gonna work with him one day. Maybe he'll play my dad,'" Adam told the online celebrity magazine *Mr. Showbiz* in June 1996. "I wish she could have seen this."

Caan and Sandler's moments together oncamera, however, were not what captured the public's attention. The one scene in the movie that fans and press would later zero in on (in the same way they had focused on Adam's fight with Bob Barker in *Happy Gilmore*) was a shower scene, almost certainly improvised by Sandler, where Adam-as-Archie serenades Wayans-as-Keats with a hilarious rendition of "I Will Always Love You," the Dolly Parton song Whitney Houston had made famous in her hit movie, *The Bodyguard* (1992).

Critics claimed to see homoerotic overtones in this sequence. Yet, as Adam's character Sonny Koufax would later point out in *Big Daddy* (1999), critics can be "cynical a**holes."

Bulletproof wrapped in April 1996. Director Dickerson took the finished footage and headed into post-production. Wayans went off to shoot *Celtic Pride* (1996), a movie which would team him with another ex-*SNL* comic, Dan Aykroyd, and another member of Sandler's seemingly ubiquitous NYU crowd, Judd Apatow, who was writing the film.

Meanwhile, Adam went off to be a rock 'n' roll star.

☽   ☽   ☽

The origins of Adam's 1996 concert tour might be traced to the experience he'd had recording his second CD, *What the Hell Happened to Me?* On that 1996 album, he'd gotten the chance to work firsthand with the cream of Los Angeles's studio musicians.

Or, it might be tracked back, even further, to his musical performances on *SNL,* and the enthusiastic reception songs such as "Red-Hooded Sweatshirt" and "The Chanukah Song" had received from studio audiences and home TV viewers.

And then, again, it might go all the way back to those school dances at Central High in Manchester, New Hampshire, when Adam stood in front of his schoolmates belting out classic 1970s and 1980s rock tunes.

Whatever his motivation, summer 1996 found Adam preparing to head out on the road with a full rock 'n' roll band, to perform not just songs from his records, but classic rock tunes also—given the special Sandler spin, of course. Adam and guitarist/ musical director Waddy Wachtel, drummer Don Heffington, bassist Bob Glaub, guitarist Teddy Castellucci, keyboardist Mike Thompson, percussionist John Rosenberg, and backup singers Mindy Abair (who doubled on saxophone), Sonetta Gibson, and Kim Schwarz began a full month of rehearsals in late April 1996.

"The band is unbelievable," Adam enthused to the *Boston Herald*'s Dean Johnson on June 14, 1996. "And I get to be the goofy frontman."

Goofy, perhaps, but unprepared, definitely not. The band rehearsed throughout May, taking one of their few breaks to play at the 1996 MTV Movie Awards in New York City, where Adam and Bob Barker had been nominated for Best Fight. Reporters covering the May 30 ceremony (co-hosted by Ben Stiller and Janeane Garofalo) got to see more of the publicity-shy Sandler that evening than they usually saw within any given month.

Adam performed with his newly named "Goat Band." He clowned with Bob Barker when the two won the award for Best Fight, and, after the ceremonies, huddled backstage with reported girlfriend Alicia Silverstone until well past midnight.

Adam's concert tour—a three-truck, four-bus multimedia extravaganza that he quickly dubbed "a backyard rock 'n' roll party for you and 5,000 of your friends"—officially launched on June 6, 1996, in Las Vegas.

The stage set designed for the show had, in fact, been built to look like a typical suburban backyard, complete with rocking chair and cabana hut. Huge video screens, which alternated between closeups of Adam and video footage geared to specific songs (a goat trapped in the back of a truck, for example), dominated either side of the stage.

The tour was full of the hijinks you'd expect from any other rock band. In Kansas City, Adam gave away a pair of boxer shorts to an enthusiastic fan. In Cincinnati he threw his red-hooded sweatshirt into the crowd and revived Cajunman for a brief visit. In Mansfield, New Hampshire, he donned a beret, sunglasses, and a gold blouse for a straight (and surprisingly sensual) rendition of Marvin Gaye's "Let's Get It On."

He and the band goofed around on the bus ("[we] started a spontaneous mosh pit, everybody flying and jumping all around," he told writer G. Brown just prior to his Denver shows), and they goofed around onstage. Gibson Guitars (makers of the red SG he'd played back in high school) had built him a special goat-shaped instrument, and he used (and abused) it every night.

Adam changed around the set order: one night, opening with "Lunchlady Land," the next with a dead-on cover of Foghat's version of "I Just Wanna Make Love to You."

Chris Farley joined Adam onstage for the June 29, 1996, performance at Chicago's Rosemont Theatre for a duet on "The Halloween Song." Allen Covert took off his actor's hat and took a turn as a stand-up comedian, serving as Adam's opening act throughout the tour.

The show lasted six weeks, at one point covering twenty-one cities in twenty-two days. On June 14, Adam was at New York City's Radio City Music Hall, just around the corner from his old *SNL* haunts. On June 17, he was back home in New Hampshire, at Mansfield's Great Woods Center for the Performing Arts. On July 8, Sandler played in Fort Worth, Texas. On July 9 and 10, he was at Denver's Paramount Theatre. The concert tour closed on July 14, 1996, at the Universal Amphitheater in Los Angeles.

Despite his arduous trek, Adam still hadn't had enough of the rock 'n' roll lifestyle.

He appeared onstage with the band White Zombie during their July 19, 1996, gig at Los Angeles's Great Western Forum, joining in (to thunderous applause from the crowd) on the song "More Human than Human."

Like everything Adam did professionally, his tour received a mixed reception from the media. "There are words to describe what happened to Sandler in Milwaukee on Tuesday night," reported critic Dave Tianen of the *Milwaukee Journal Sentinel.* "Words like tanked. Bombed. Bellyflopped." "A couple of cuddly songs don't make a show," insisted Dave Ferman of the *Fort Worth* (Texas) *Star-Telegram.*

The Boston Herald, in contrast, found "genuine cleverness" in Sandler's song renditions. The *Patriot-Ledger* out of Quincy, Massachusetts, thought the program's "goofy, good-natured vibe" hard to resist. "His mere presence elicits laughter and fun," described Brian Magnarini in the *Cincinnati Enquirer.*

As the opening act, Allen Covert's reviews ran the spectrum as well, from lukewarm ("Covert is not awful, but there are better comics playing Milwaukee clubs any weekend") to scathing ("If you want really, pitifully bad comedy, opener Allen Covert is your man"), to damning with faint praise ("straightforward and amusing stand-up").

None of the criticism affected Adam.

"The show's just intended for people to kick back," he told Dean Johnson of the *Boston Herald* on June 14, 1996. "It has a party feel, and [I try] to make [them] laugh, dance, and have fun."

When the party was over (HBO cable aired Adam's Chicago appearance as a special on October 11, 1996), Sandler went back to moviemaking.

○   ○   ○

"My feeling was people would pay their $7.50 [at the multiplex box office] to see Damon [Wayans] and Adam [Sandler] and laugh . . . [they'd] walk away liking the action and liking the story but really sort of relishing the chemistry between Damon and Adam," said *Bulletproof* producer Robert Simonds to the *Hollywood Reporter* on September 11, 1996.

Simonds was at least partially right. Released to 2,240 theaters on September 6, 1996, *Bulletproof* (on an admittedly weak box-office weekend) took the top slot, grossing $6 million.

Critical reaction to the picture was so mixed as to be almost schizophrenic. Hal Hinson of the *Washington Post* decided, "A bullet in the head would be less painful than suffering through this formulaic parade of chase scenes," while Desson Howe of the same paper termed the movie, "Rambunctious, crude, ridiculous, violent, and—incidentally—very funny." To Joe Leydon (*Houston Press*), *Bulletproof* was "the sort of guilty pleasure that should be savored in a crowded theater on a Saturday night, with a giant tub of popcorn and a total lack of inhibition." For Lisa Schwarzbaum (*Entertainment Weekly*) it was a "gutless comedy" and full of "formulaic drivel." Leonard Klady (*Variety*) rated the new offering as "Strictly programmer fare" and analyzed, "The criminal activity onscreen . . . is penny ante compared with the felonious slaughter of story, character and logic exacted by the pic's filmmakers."

Reviewers were also split on the entertainment value of the screen pairing of Sandler and Wayans. "This is a buddy movie starring two people who have absolutely no chemistry between them," declared New York City's *Village Voice*. A bit farther uptown, Stephen Holden of the *New York Times* wrote "Sandler and Wayans . . . glint off each other as they josh their way through the dumber-than-dumb story of a singularly embattled friendship."

The most vituperative reaction came from *Time* magazine. In an article titled "The Next Worst Thing" (and subtitled: "Like Him or Not, Adam Sandler Isn't Going Away"), critic Richard Corliss proclaimed that "[Sandler's] Cajunman, Operaman and the rest were not varied characters; they were expressions of one capacious ego. The issue for him was not selling out but finding a buyer." *Variety*'s Leonard Klady insisted, "Sandler seems woefully out of place. His puppy-dog quality gets tiresome quickly in the action setting and strains one's belief in an innate ability to dodge bullets."

Adam's *Bulletproof* performance—particularly the controversial shower scene—did have its fans: "When Sandler cuts loose with a serenely insane version of 'I Will Always Love You' . . . the lunacy reaches a level of inspiration that Eddie Murphy often achieved in the original *48 Hours* (1982)," Leydon of the *Houston Press* stated in his critique. Roger Ebert was even more emphatic in his praise.

On the Sunday, September 8, 1996, edition of TV's *Siskel and Ebert,* he declared, "This film redeems Adam Sandler." Ebert went on to say that he felt both Wayans and Sandler did a good job in the movie, but that the material betrayed them. Michael Rechstaffen of the *Hollywood Reporter,* in giving the picture a 'C-,' concurred, pointing out the film's "threadbare story line."

Of all the evaluations of Adam and *Bulletproof,* Ebert and Rechstaffen were the most perceptive. The screenplay seems to go through the motions of characterization, and, despite their protestations to the contrary, much of the film does feel like Wayans and Sandler riffing off of each other.

Simonds had been correct about one thing: Enough Sandler/ Wayans fans showed up for the picture to earn back its reported $24.5 million budget (the movie took in $21 million at the box-office, and another $26.7 million from video rentals). *Bulletproof,* however, was not the "franchise-creating" picture (as Mel Gibson and Danny Glover's *Lethal Weapon* films had been) he and Universal had been hoping for. A crucial point demonstrated by this film was that to put Adam Sandler in an R-rated feature was to deny a percentage of his under-eighteen-year-old faithful followers the chance to see him on the big screen.

The movie's relatively modest box-office performance, however, failed to dim Adam's star in the industry's eyes. He and Ben Stiller were rumored to be set to star as brothers at the time of the American Civil War who open the nation's first Holiday Inn, in a movie to be produced by actor/filmmaker Danny DeVito. (This project has yet to materialize.)

And, as the December 4, 1996, issue of *Variety* reported, New Line Cinema had purchased a script to be co-written by Sandler's friend Judd Apatow and TV's *NewsRadio* (1995–99) staff writer Drake Sather, a love story between a working class New Hampshire man and a gorgeous movie star.

Adam, so the trade journal reported, was not "contractually attached to the project, but [planned to] work closely with Apatow and Sather on developing the script."

Although neither of those projects have come to pass as of this writing, the end of the year did bring intriguing news regarding Adam's other New Line Cinema project—*The Wedding Band.*

A lead female role had been added to the production. Drew Barrymore, one of the world's hottest and hippest young actresses, had been cast in this key assignment. Carrie Fisher, who, since her days as Princess Leia of the *Star Wars* trilogy (1977–83) had become known for her deft screenwriting hand, came aboard to add her magic touch to the screenplay (which had received a new title since it had last made news).

Adam's next feature film was now called *The Wedding Singer,* and it was scheduled to begin shooting in February 1997.

CHAPTER 9

going to the chapel

"We tried to make it as sweet as possible,

or as sweet as I could be."

ADAM SANDLER,

talking about *The Wedding Singer,* 1997

THE NEW YEAR BROUGHT ADAM SANDLER two new film projects. In February 1997, he signed a deal (for an undisclosed seven-figure sum) with another studio that had been aggressively pursuing him, Disney's Touchstone Pictures, for *The Waterboy* (1998). Sandler and Tim Herlihy's pitch concerned a college football team's "water distribution engineer," who turns out to be a devastatingly effective player, with hilarious consequences. Herlihy—who had recently been named *Saturday Night Live*'s head writer—was to write the script.

Another of Adam's old friends working on a movie script at the time was actor Peter Berg. Since his role in 1989's *Going*

Overboard (where he was disguised under a hat and sunglasses), Berg had gone on to costar (1995–99) on the CBS-TV medical drama, *Chicago Hope,* as a free-spirited youngish physician. Berg's screenplay was a dark comedy concerning friends who come together for a bachelor party, where things get very much out of hand.

Berg had not only written the script; he planned to make it his feature film directorial debut. In March 1997, Adam helped out Peter by doing an industry reading of the screenplay with actors Christian Slater and Robert Patrick. The performance created quite a buzz around town and made *Very Bad Things* one of the season's hottest properties. Polygram acquired the screen rights, and Adam planned to be part of the cast when the project was made.

While he was busy planning out his future, Adam had not forgotten about his past. On March 3, 1997, he participated in a twenty-eight-person salute to *Saturday Night Live* at the U.S. Comedy Festival in Aspen. He joined producer Lorne Michaels and fellow *SNL* vets Dana Carvey, Chevy Chase, Chris Farley, Jon Lovitz, Steve Martin, and Martin Short (among many, many others) in a heartfelt tribute that lasted well over two hours and wrapped up the festival, appropriately enough, on a Saturday night. He and several others ended the night at Pinon's, Aspen's top restaurant (according to Zagat's restaurant guide), where Adam charmed diners and staffers alike by walking into the kitchen when the meal was over to praise the chefs.

Then it was back to work for Adam, on a project which, coincidentally enough, would also find him paying tribute, once again, to the past.

When Drew Barrymore had joined *The Wedding Singer* in December 1996, the project took a quantum leap up the Hollywood "visibility ladder." Though by no means yet an A-list star, she was from a far different world than Adam's usual cast of co-players. For example, Damon Wayans may have shared top billing with Adam on *Bulletproof* (1996), but in the eyes of the mainstream press, they were cut from the same cloth: that is, they were comedians and entertainment personalities first and foremost, not actors. And, although James Caan and Carl Weathers of the same picture had certainly been in their share of high-profile screen projects over the years, their glory days were past. Barrymore, on the other hand and as most observers agreed, was just entering hers.

The granddaughter of the late stage and screen great John Barrymore, as well as the goddaughter of filmmaker Steven Spielberg, Drew was the closest thing Hollywood had to royalty. She'd made her first commercial before she was two years old, her big-screen debut at age four (as William Hurt's daughter in 1980's *Altered States*), and had been in the public eye since her turn as Gertie in Spielberg's *E.T. The Extra Terrestrial* (1982). In 1997, at the age of twenty-three, she'd already packed enough excitement into her life to write a book—which she had, in fact, already done.

Her best-selling autobiography, *Little Girl Lost* (published when she was all of sixteen), had given the world a peek at what life in the Hollywood fast lane was sometimes like. The pages were filled with the celebrity's narrative of her drug and alcohol abuse, her year-long stint in a mental health facility, and her troubled relationship with her famous family. More recently, her outrageous antics (a three-week-long marriage that ended in divorce, a photo layout for *Playboy* magazine, flashing her breasts at David Letterman while as a guest on his late-night TV talk show), and her show business comeback, in films such as *Poison Ivy* (1992), *The Amy Fisher Story* (a 1992 telefeature), and *Scream* (1996), had caught the public's attention.

Her presence in *The Wedding Singer* gave the upcoming movie an instant cachet. Press coverage of the project reflected its new profile. *Entertainment Tonight,* the popular syndicated television gossip show, for example, did a special report from the set on February 11, 1997, early in the movie's shooting, a full year before *The Wedding Singer*'s scheduled release.

Not only did Drew lend the forthcoming film star power, at Adam's invitation, she also brought her experienced eye to bear on the movie's narrative. The two had several discussions regarding their onscreen characters, and their ideas were subsequently incorporated into rewrites of Tim Herlihy's initial draft. Adam, Carrie Fisher, and finally, writer Judd Apatow all lent (an uncredited) hand in shaping the final screenplay.

In the finished plot line, Adam plays Robbie Hart, the wedding singer of the title, who as the story opens is left at the altar by his long-time girlfriend, Linda. Linda is disgusted with the way Robbie's life has turned out—he's gone from being the lead singer of a rock band to bunking out in his sister's basement and making a living of sorts singing clichéd tunes at tacky weddings.

With Linda's departure, the normally sunny Robbie turns bitter and depressed; his moods carry over to his wedding performances. About the only bright spot in his humdrum existence is a new friendship with a perky waitress named Julia (Drew Barrymore) who is herself engaged to be married. Robbie discovers her intended is a duplicitous cad—and, in the process, realizes he loves her. After a series of misunderstandings, the couple find themselves together on a plane heading for Las Vegas—and their own wedding ceremony.

The usual behind-the-scenes crew was on tap for *The Wedding Singer:* Robert Simonds and Jack Giarraputo produced; Sandy Wernick and Brad Grey were executive producers. Allen Covert returned, in his biggest part yet, as Sammy, Robbie's limousine-driving best pal. Actress Christine Taylor, best known for her role as Marcia Brady in *The Brady Bunch Movie* (1995) and *A Very Brady Sequel* (1996), played Holly, Julia's cousin.

There were parts for *SNL* alumni Kevin Nealon, Bob Smigel, Jon Lovitz (in an uncredited role as one of Robbie's rival wedding crooners), and Angela Featherstone, producer Simonds's then fiancée (appearing as Robbie's intended, Linda). Matthew Glave (noted for his recurring role as Dr. Dale Edson in the late 1990s TV series *ER*) played Julia's betrothed, Glenn Gulia.

Robbie's oncamera wedding band included Teddy Castellucci as the guitar player, and Alexis Arquette, who did a very real Boy George impersonation as the group's keyboard player. Steve Buscemi provided an uncredited turn during the movie's opening sequence as a drunken toastmaster, and Billy Idol did a cameo as himself at the finale. Involved in a Sandler film for the first time was Adam's onetime New York University dormmate Frank Coraci, making his major studio directorial debut with *The Wedding Singer*. During Adam's *SNL* stint (1991–95), while Giarraputo and Herlihy were attending law school, Coraci was circling the globe, working on travel documentaries, perfecting the filmmaker's craft he had studied at NYU. In 1994, drawing on every favor he could and charging his credit cards to the maximum limit, Coraci made his first feature film, *Murdered*

Innocence. The noir thriller won Best Feature Film, Best Screenplay, and Best Directorial Debut at the Long Island Film Festival. Tom Lewis—another one of Adam's NYU dormmates, and one of Coraci's best friends—worked on *Murdered Innocence* as film editor, and now joined *The Wedding Singer* crew in that same capacity.

With all those NYU alumni—Sandler, Giarraputo, Herlihy, Coraci, Covert, Lewis, and Apatow—running around, the set at times had the air of old home week. And thanks to a critical decision made by writer Tim Herlihy early in the writing process, it had the look of Adam's schooldays as well.

"It kind of took the corniness out of me singing songs," Sandler related to writer Elias Stimac of *Drama-Logue* in early 1998. "I couldn't sing '90s tunes without people thinking, *Why is he doing that? I just heard that song on the radio.*"

It was Herlihy's idea to set the plot line in the 1980s, which not only removed the corniness that Adam talked about, but also provided the picture with seemingly limitless opportunities to poke fun at the excesses of the "Me decade." From hairstyles to clothes, from fads such as Rubik's Cube and break dancing to stars such as Madonna and Michael Jackson, no target seemed to escape the screenwriter's pen.

It was up to production designer Perry Andelin Blake and costume designer Mona May to make the 1980s come alive again onscreen. Blake had worked for Simonds's previous films *Billy Madison* (1995), *Happy Gilmore* (1996), and *Bulletproof* (1996), as well as Stephen Kessler's *Birch Street Gym* (1991). In turn, May had been part of the 1990s film and television versions of *Clueless,* as well as music videos for Axl Rose, Run DMC, and Luther Vandross.

One of the first production decisions made was to put a wig on Adam, to give his screen character a hairstyle more appropriate to that bygone decade. "[That] was not fun," Adam later told *People Online.* "They had to put that wig on me every day and take it off. I remember I ripped it off a few times and they yelled at me because that rips the netting."

Big hair aside, Adam (and Drew, for that matter) emerged relatively unscathed, sartorially speaking. The film's real fashion victims were co-players Christine Taylor and Allen Covert. Taylor, for one, had fun creating her character's look.

"We had done a lot of pre-wardrobe planning about my costumes," Christine told *Drama-Logue*'s Elias Stimac. "Each day I would go into my trailer and the wardrobe people would have the basic shell of what I was wearing that day. But the accessories— that's what it was all about! The rosary beads and the bracelets and the lace gloves and earrings and ribbons. I could pick and choose all my own accessories, which was very exciting."

The look that emerged was very Madonna-esque—a lot of bustiers and lace—which was very much in keeping with Holly's party-loving movie character. Covert's wardrobe was just as flamboyant.

"I was a walking ad for the '80s. . . . I had shoulder pads, sleeveless shirts, mesh, parachute pants, pinkie rings, earrings— any crazy thing anyone ever saw in the '80s, they gave to me," the comic told online entertainment guide *Hollywood.com.* Covert didn't mention his most memorable outfit: a red and black leather costume that was identical to the one Michael

Jackson had sported in the high-profile "Thriller" video. Further aping Jackson's 1980s look, Covert wore a single white glove with the outfit.

It wasn't just the clothes that made the movie look so authentically 1980s, director Frank Coraci revealed in the same interview. "Everything [then] was man-made, so we used mixtures of teal and pink or purple and yellow—combinations you haven't seen since the '80s."

The director used color in other ways as well. The colors at each of the occasions Robbie sings change from pastel tones to more somber ones as the singer's mood darkens in the narrative.

Most of the plot line marriage ceremonies were shot in the old Ambassador Hotel on Wilshire Boulevard in Los Angeles— under very inflexible deadlines. Despite the movie's $28 million budget, *The Wedding Singer* was filmed in a tight thirty-four days—roughly half the average industry length today. Producer Robert Simonds explained one rather unique way they devised to save time—and money.

"While we shoot one [ceremony], we're prepping another one 100 yards away," Simonds told writer Patrick Goldstein of the *Los Angeles Times* in May 1997. "That way we can turn the camera around and shoot the next scene without moving to another location."

Setting the film in the past also eased one of Simonds's major concerns regarding the entire "Wedding Singer" concept. After the lukewarm reception *Bulletproof* had received, the producer wanted to ensure Sandler fans would show up in force for his next movie.

"We were worried about Adam's core audience being turned off by Adam in a romantic comedy," Simonds admitted to writer

Amy Wallace of the *Los Angeles Times* in February 1998. "By sticking it back in 1985, it mitigated the problem." (The nostalgia aspect of *The Wedding Singer* proved to be so strong that it gave the film an appeal all its own.)

There was another creative problem, however, that Simonds wasn't addressing. If (as New Line Cinema and producer Simonds kept insisting) this was the production that was going to substantially expand Adam Sandler's audience, he had to be a credible leading man. Would Adam be able to create an onscreen character with whom Drew Barrymore's heroine could believably fall in love? Or would he come off as Canteen Boy in a bad wig? (Adam would later elaborate to *E! Online* about the challenge at hand: "The ultimate goal was to make people laugh, but my character had to be believably in love. You have to believe that this guy wants to be with this woman and that he's got some pain because he can't be with her. I didn't want to only make fun of that.")

Almost exactly a year after its release in February 1996, Adam's second album, *What the Hell Happened to Me?* went platinum, achieving sales of more than one million copies. Just as impressive was the fact that in February 1997 the release was still selling more than 5,000 units a week. (As had his first, Sandler's second CD was nominated for a Grammy Award. At the February 26, 1997, awards ceremony, however, at the Shrine Auditorium in Los Angeles, it was *Rush Limbaugh Is a Big Fat Idiot*—featuring Al Franken—that won the prize in the Best Spoken Comedy Album category.)

Inspired by the reaction to his "Backyard Barbecue" tour, Adam had gone right back into the studio with his band and producer Brooks Arthur to produce his third comedy album, *What's Your Name?* (1997). Unlike his previous two Warner Bros. releases, this record (which featured a picture of Adam in black and white face paint, á la the rock group KISS, on the album's cover) had *no* comedy sketches on it. The disc's fifteen tracks were musical parodies, similar to what Weird Al Yankovic does, with the exception that Sandler's tunes were all original songs. Was the new approach too much of a stretch? Not according to producer Arthur.

"He's a wonderful singer," Brooks related in an interview for Warner Bros.' online Adam Sandler Web site. "That's why I love working with him. He can sing the heck out of a song. The other day he sang me 'If I Loved You,' from *Carousel*. John Raitt [Bonnie's father, who'd made the song famous on Broadway in the mid-1940s] would have been proud."

Raitt might have been Arthur's reference point, but it's clear in listening to the album that, for Adam, the artists whose styles he used as a point of departure were more modern ones. "The Lonesome Kicker" evokes mid-1980s Bruce Springsteen, while "Pickin' Daisies" (with its prominent, Beatle-like sitar part) mirrors classic 1960s pop.

Other tracks on *What's Your Name?* included "The Goat Song" (which finally revealed the life story of Adam's favorite barnyard animal), "Sweet Beatrice," and "Moyda"—the funk-infused account of a sympathetic serial killer. The album closed with Adam's old *SNL* favorite "Red-Hooded Sweatshirt," done as a piano and guitar ballad.

In preparation for the CD's release, Adam did a round of concert appearances in late summer and early fall 1997 with multi-instrumentalist Teddy Castellucci and drummer Don

Huffner: For the most part, they played college campuses around the United States.

Adam also went to NFL Films to produce an authentic-looking video for "The Lonesome Kicker," which was to be the album's first single. Shot at Pittsburgh's Three Rivers Stadium, the short film featured Frank Coraci (wearing Pittsburgh Steeler uniform number 8) as the kicker—Andre Kristacovitchalinski Jr.

In the video, Coraci stoically endured the taunts of his teammates, waiting for his chance in the spotlight, while Sandler played guitar and, putting himself in Kristacovitchalinski's shoes, sang of the kicker's "tough" lot in life. Watching the finished video now, one is struck by the many similarities between "The Lonesome Kicker" character and Bobby Boucher of *The Waterboy*, which would begin shooting in early 1998.

MTV premiered "The Lonesome Kicker" in September 1997—right around the time Adam appeared as a presenter at the annual Music Videos Awards, hosted by his buddy comedian/actor Chris Rock.

The full CD, *What's Your Name?*, was launched in record stores September 16, 1997. In Los Angeles, both the Virgin Megastore and the Tower Records emporium on Sunset Boulevard in West Hollywood did huge window displays of Adam and the album. Sandler made appearances on TV's *Late Night with Conan O'Brien* and *The Late Show with David Letterman* to promote the CD.

What's Your Name? gathered the by-now traditional mixed reception: that is, the star's fans adored it, while most critics remained perplexed by Adam's growing appeal.

E! Online graded the record a "D-," calling it "a bad Bob Seger record—with fewer laughs . . . as Sandler gets more musically proficient, his skit-rock grows lyrically anemic." *The Denver*

Rocky Mountain News liked it a little better, giving the record a "C+": "Adam Sandler albums are a lot like his movies: You can stomach about ten minutes of each," decided reviewer Michael Mehle. On the other hand, Jeff MacDonald, writing for the *Daily Texan* out of Austin, enthused, "*What's Your Name?* will have you rolling on the floor by the second track.

Sandler confirms on [this record] that he is a trailblazing comedic force to be reckoned with, still one of the brightest funnymen of his generation."

Michael Corcoran of the *Austin* (Texas) *American-Statesman* was particularly impressed by the high level of musicianship displayed on the record, not just by the sidemen, but by Sandler as well. "[He] seems to have approached this album as a songwriter first, and as a comedian second. . . . The yucks are more satisfying when they're surrounded by so much craftsmanship and cleverness." Corcoran rated the record three-and-a-half out of a possible four stars.

Though *What's Your Name?* would end up spending seventeen weeks on *Billboard*'s Album chart, it never achieved the breakout success of Adam's first two entries. Fans and reviewers alike bemoaned the lack of new comedy routines, new Sandler characters á la "Tollbooth Willie" and "Mr. Bake-O." Though no one seemed to mind the combination of music and comedy, Adam's fans wanted him front and center, not buried in a glossy, full-on rock 'n' roll production. They were about to get their wish, in spades.

○   ○   ○

"Adam Sandler is one of the most creative and talented comics performing today, who has attracted quite a following from moviegoers worldwide. ShowEast is pleased to honor such a young and talented performer so early in his career." With those words, uttered in October 1997, Greg Dunn (general chairman of ShowEast, an association of East Coast movie theater owners) announced that Adam had been selected Comedy Star of the Year by the organization. The award would be presented to Adam at the Trump Taj Mahal in Atlantic City, during the theater owners' annual convention.

New Line Cinema made plans to screen *The Wedding Singer* at ShowEast. And in a marketing stunt that typified the creative approach the company would take throughout the film's promotion, it arranged for Adam to make an appearance in character immediately after the film's showing. The occasion? The real-life wedding of New Line's distribution district manager Michelle Indick and her fiancé Andrew Gurland.

"Andrew and I are major Adam Sandler fans," Indick told *Variety* reporter Monica Roman. "We watched him on *Saturday Night Live* and we've seen all his movies."

Immediately after the actual ceremony (the couple was married by Atlantic City Mayor James Whalen), Adam sang "Always and Forever" to the happy bride and groom, and the fifteen hundred guests New Line had invited to the dinnertime occasion.

Right after ShowEast, additional confirmation of Adam's fast-rising show-business star appeared in the news. On November 7, 1997, noted show-business columnist Army Archer reported in *Daily Variety* that director Martin Scorcese and screenwriter Nicholas Pileggi were putting together a movie based on the life of Dean Martin, focusing on Martin's swinging years with the fabled Rat Pack in the 1950s and thereafter. Tom Hanks was slated to play Martin, John Travolta would be Frank Sinatra,

Jim Carrey as Jerry Lewis, Hugh Grant as actor Peter Lawford, and playing the role of comedian Joey Bishop, Archer reported, would be . . . Adam Sandler. (To date, this intriguing project remains on the drawing board.)

As 1997 drew to a close, all the signs pointed to continued—possibly even breakout—success for Adam in 1998. The coming year, it seemed, would be a great one. That is, until one December evening that changed all that.

"I'm not comfortable being around too many people. I don't like being out in public too much. I don't like going to bars. I don't like doing celebrity stuff."

That's Adam Sandler, talking with *E! Online* about how he liked to devote his free time. Yet, although he was content to remain out of the spotlight, among his generation of actors, he was very much the exception to the rule. The lure of the fast lane proved too much for many. Peter Berg's upcoming *Very Bad Things,* which Adam had committed to earlier in the year, took a step back in the production process late in 1997 when that film's star Christian Slater was arrested and sent to a drug rehabilitation center. Ex-*SNL* player/actor Robert Downey Jr. was in the news as much for his ongoing drug problem as his many films. (One of the most famous casualties of the "fast-lane" lifestyle had been original *SNL* Not Ready for Prime Time player John Belushi, who died in 1981 of a heroin-and-cocaine overdose in a Beverly Hills Hotel bungalow.)

In December 1997, the excesses and pressures so often associated with Hollywood stardom took the life of yet another ex-*SNL* comedian, one who had always considered John Belushi his idol.

Thirty-three-year-old Chris Farley was found dead in a Chicago apartment—a week before Christmas—of what police would later determine was a drug overdose.

Adam was devastated.

"I have never gone through this before," Adam later expressed to writer Janet Weeks of *USA Today*. "I had grandparents pass away, and that hurts a lot. But that's natural. This is an unnatural death. And I can't stop thinking about it."

Chris Farley's funeral took place on December 23, 1997, in his hometown of Madison, Wisconsin. Adam was there, as were Lorne Michaels, and *SNL* alumni including Dan Aykroyd, Chris Rock, Rob Schneider, and Al Franken. (Farley's frequent onscreen partner, David Spade, was simply too upset to attend.)

The occasion was marked, as Farley's brother Tom would tell *USA Today*, "in typical Irish fashion: a lot of tears, a lot of laughter." The ceremony was as true to Farley's spirit as could be fashioned under the circumstances. During the services, a priest described the day Chris showed up for rugby practice in a pink polo shirt and plaid shorts, and the back of the funeral program featured the specially written "A Clown's Prayer," an invocation to bring more joy than tears to the world.

Despite their closeness over recent years, Adam had never been able to pull his friend completely away from the demons that drove him. Where the passage of time had provided Sandler with perspective on his growing stardom, Farley was never able to achieve a similar sense of inner peace.

"Chris, like a lot of comedians, had high ups and low downs," Adam told Elias Stimac of *Drama-Logue*. "When I would hang with him, I mostly saw ups, and when he was down, we would talk and try to get him up again."

Adam experienced real pain for not being able to buoy Farley through his last rough patch, and he felt deeply for Chris's family. "It happened so close to Christmas, and they [are] very religious," he told the Internet's *Hollywood.com*. "I know it's going to be a mess every Christmas for them."

Besides the pain, there was also a sense of unfinished business, Chris's cameo appearance in *Billy Madison* aside. Adam and Chris had never found the right time to work together on a film project.

For a long time to come, the loss of his close friend would haunt Adam. It would color the success that, as 1998 approached, waited just around the corner for Sandler.

CHAPTER 10

the big breakout

"Humor and intellect make the best combination

in a human being, and Adam's got them both."

DREW BARRYMORE, 1998

NO MATTER HOW THEY FELT ABOUT HIS WORK as an entertainer, no critic could impugn Adam Sandler's loyalty to his friends. In the late 1980s, Stephen Kessler had given Adam work by casting the then-struggling young actor in commercials the director was doing. A few years later, Sandler turned right around and pushed Kessler forward to direct *Billy Madison* (1995). In addition, Sandler arranged a role for his New York University classmate Allen Covert in 1989's *Going Overboard*. Adam maneuvered a two-week audition for Tim Herlihy on *Saturday Night Live's* writing staff in the early 1990s. Today, Jack Giarraputo, Frank Coraci, and Tom Lewis, as well, owe, if not their success (too much money is at stake in the motion picture business to get by without real talent), then the opportunities they subsequently received in the industry to Adam Sandler.

Actor Peter Berg (*The Last Seduction, Copland*) was one of Sandler's pals too. That's why Adam had done the reading in early 1997 for Berg's self-written script of *Very Bad Things* in the first place, and this is the reason Adam had agreed, in principle, to do the movie. When Christian Slater, the film's star, went into rehab for his drug problem and the picture was postponed, Adam's support for the project remained unflagging.

In late 1997, Slater was now a free man, clean and sober, and anxious to begin work on the picture. So was director Berg.

Adam, however, was having second thoughts.

In *Very Bad Things,* he would be playing a killer, and, even though the death he causes is accidental, a very unsympathetic character. He began to think the part was too much of a departure and stretch for him. In the same way his audience had not accepted him as a heroin dealer in *Bulletproof* (1996), his fans might well be turned off seeing him in another negative screen role.

Then, too, the recent death of Adam's friend Chris Farley may very well have played a part in Sandler's thinking. Perhaps the last thing he wanted in his life at that point in time was more death. Thus, at the last minute, in what was a very difficult career decision, Sandler backed out of Berg's film.

"Adam was great in rehearsals, but said he just couldn't do it," Peter Berg later told the online magazine *Mr. Showbiz.* "It was just too dark for him."

(The comedy-thriller was eventually shot, with Adam's role going to Jeremy Piven, best known as costar of TV's *Ellen* in the mid-1990s. When released in 1998, *Very Bad Things* received very bad reviews and very little box office—less than $10 million.)

Once he withdrew from Berg's film, Adam was free to begin work on Touchstone's *The Waterboy*, which began shooting in Florida in January 1998.

Once again, the movie set was like old home week.

The major behind-the-scenes names from *The Wedding Singer* (1998) were all back on board for *The Waterboy*: director Frank Coraci, screenwriter Tim Herlihy, producers Jack Giarraputo and Robert Simonds, production designer Perry Andelin Blake, and film editor Tom Lewis. There was also a new name (albeit a familiar one) in the production credits: Adam Sandler was listed as the film's executive producer.

As the narrative opens, Adam's character—Bobby Boucher, the waterboy of the title—is fired from his job as "water distribution engineer" for the University of Louisiana after eighteen years of loyal service. The simplistic soul soon joins another football team—the Mud Dogs. Under the weak-willed supervision of head coach Klein, however, the Mud Dogs have lost forty gridiron games in a row.

When some of the squad pick on the newcomer—and more importantly, his carefully arranged variety of water refreshments (rain, tap, and bottled)—Bobby goes ballistic and fights back. He tackles one particularly malicious heckler with such abandon that Coach Klein asks him to repeat the move. When Bobby does so, the coach realizes he's got a potential new star on his hands.

Klein visits Bobby's house in the bayou country to convince Mama Boucher to allow her thirty-year-old boy to play ball. She, however, doesn't like the idea.

Mama also doesn't approve of Vicki Vallencourt, Bobby's childhood girlfriend who has just gotten out of jail. Vicki encourages Bobby to stand up for himself, and he does, joining the team against Mama's wishes. The Mud Dogs begin to pile up victory after victory, led by Boucher's amazing defensive athletic feats. All this success turns sour, however, when Mama finds out Bobby has lied to her about playing ball and collapses. She's taken to the hospital and Bobby, blaming himself for her illness, stops playing football. In the end, however, Mama relents and her offspring, Bobby, reaches the stadium just in time to lead the Mud Dogs to success in the Whiskey Bowl.

Location scouts for *The Waterboy* had been hard at work in central Florida since the end of 1997, trying to rent studio space for the production to shoot its interior scenes. Another Touchstone entry, the Anthony Hopkins/Cuba Gooding Jr. psychological thriller *Instinct* (1999) was occupying Disney-MGM studios in Lake Buena Vista, Florida, so *The Waterboy*, a Disney production, ended up renting space at Universal Studios in Orlando.

The scouts had better luck finding exteriors: a football field in De Land, Florida (some twenty-five miles north of Orlando) became the Mud Dogs' home stadium, a boat launch along an inland waterway in De Bary (ten miles south of De Land) served as the Bouchers' bayou shack, and the Citrus Bowl in Orlando (filled with eight thousand extras) became the site for the movie's climactic Whiskey Bowl contest.

Yet, although the scouts were hard at work, so were Florida's infamous hurricanes. A series of severe storms in January 1998 delayed shooting more than once, and, even worse, they did serious damage to many area residences. In response, Adam and *The Waterboy* crew led a fund and clothing drive to assist those in need.

The production had other visitors besides the bad weather. Adam's parents, who lived nearby, stopped by to observe their famous son at work. "Mom wasn't familiar with the etiquette on the set," Adam would later tell David Letterman on TV's *Late Night*. "She was very loud . . . [she kept asking] 'is that the real house or did they build it for the movie?'"

Adam's parents picked the right movie to peer in on, at least in terms of star power. The supporting cast boasted many big names in show business: Oscar-winning Kathy Bates as Mama Boucher, Henry Winkler as Coach Klein, Fairuza Balk as Vicki Vallencourt, and Jerry Reed (costar in all of Burt Reynolds's *Smokey and the Bandit* entries) as Coach Red Beaulieu, Bobby Boucher's arch-nemesis.

Allen Covert played one of the Mud Dogs' two biggest fans, Walter (the other, Paco, was performed by Ron Howard's brother, Clint). *SNL* alumnus Rob Schneider was also in the film, in an uncredited role as the townie who kept yelling "You can do it!" to Bobby.

And, in yet another testament to Adam's loyalty to his friends, Chris Farley's brothers, Kevin and John, had minor roles in the proceedings.

The completed eighty-nine-minute picture also featured cameos from gridiron greats Lawrence Taylor, Lynn Swann, and Dan Fouts. In addition, there were two real-life National Football League coaches on tap in *The Waterboy*: the Pittsburgh Steelers' Bill Cowher (on whom, Winkler joked, he'd based the character of Coach Klein) and the Miami Dolphins' Jimmy Johnson.

Moreover, the comedy found onscreen moments for two real-life TV sports commentators: Dan Patrick and Brent Musburger.

Sandler and Herlihy had created Mama Boucher with Kathy Bates in mind, but weren't sure she'd be interested. In fact, the performer's initial inclination was to say no to the offer. "It didn't seem like my kind of movie," she later told *Entertainment Weekly* (August 17, 1998). "I didn't know much about Adam Sandler, but my niece said, 'He's fabulous. You have to do this.' I took a hard look at the script and found myself laughing hysterically."

The laughter continued when the shoot began: Fairuza Balk—best known for her role as one of the teenagers dabbling in witchcraft in 1996's *The Craft*—spoke to the Internet's *Hollywood.com* about the relaxed air during the making of this picture. "Many times on [a] film, when things get stressful, everything gets really quiet and people get really snappy. But it didn't happen on this set. All of the filmmakers are hilarious."

For Adam, one of the highlights of making *The Waterboy* was the opportunity to share screen time with Henry Winkler— a.k.a. "The Fonz." As the leather-jacketed Henry Fonzarelli, on TV's *Happy Days* (1974–83), Winkler won two consecutive Golden Globe Awards (in 1976 and 1977) for Best Comic Actor, received three Emmy nominations, and eventually, a star on the Hollywood Walk of Fame. The leather jacket he wore became an American icon (it's now inventoried at the Smithsonian Museum in Washington, DC, where it will eventually become part of a display on American popular culture). The character he played became a hero to a whole generation of TV viewers . . . including Adam Sandler.

"There is Fonzie memorabilia in the cabinets at Adam's house—eight-track cassettes and other assorted things," Winkler revealed in a November 1998 interview with the *Los Angeles Times*. "I was told he wanted me to come and do this thing and I said fine. My children were ecstatic."

Shooting for *The Waterboy* began in January and continued through March 1998. Simultaneously, New Line Cinema began its marketing campaign for *The Wedding Singer*, in preparation for that movie's February 13 release date.

From the moment Drew Barrymore joined *The Wedding Singer*, producer Robert Simonds and New Line Cinema understood they had something different, a property that could potentially bring a whole new segment of the moviegoing public to an Adam Sandler screen comedy. The challenge for the picture was not to appeal to women, as some declared, because Adam already had plenty of female fans who gladly paid to buy his records or to see him in concert. The new goal was to attract older filmgoers—female and male alike—into sampling an Adam Sandler movie. These were people who didn't know his records, who hadn't gone to his concerts or seen his previous movies, who knew Sandler, if at all, from his *Saturday Night Live* days.

At the same time they wanted to reach out to this potential new audience, New Line and Simonds were well aware that the film's basic story line—Adam Sandler, a.k.a. Canteen Boy, a.k.a. Mr. Bake-O, a.k.a. Happy Gilmore, as a sensitive Wedding Singer—ran the risk of alienating his hard-core fans.

The solution? A very focused marketing campaign, one that attempted to touch on all the film's potential audiences, by targeting each segment individually.

Robert Simonds explained the strategy in a February 23, 1998, interview with the *Los Angeles Times*. "We would carpet bomb [saturate] the specific demographic . . . [hit] MTV with a young male [TV advertising] spot. Attack Thursday nights on NBC [home, at the time, to urban, sophisticated TV sitcoms such as *Seinfeld* and *Friends*] with mixed spots. Hit your *Suddenly Susan* and *Caroline in the City* with older female spots."

The mixed marketing strategy extended beyond television to print. Because newspaper readers tend to be older, ads in that medium played on a sense of nostalgia for the 1980s. "Before the Internet, before cell phones, before roller-blades, there was a time . . . 1985. Don't pretend you don't remember."

As Friday, February 13, 1998—the scheduled date for the picture's opening—approached, the filmmakers felt they had clearly covered all their bases. Yet they were still concerned. In retrospect, 1996's *Bulletproof* had failed because it cast Sandler against screen type. "I think people wanted to see Adam play a heroin dealer about as much as they wanted to see Jim Carrey as a cable TV repairman," Simonds told reporter Patrick Goldstein of the *Los Angeles Times* back in May 1997, referring to Carrey's relatively unsuccessful *The Cable Guy* (1996).

Would Adam's audience want to see him as a wedding singer?

After waiting more than a year while the project reached the end of post-production, it was time for all concerned to find out.

○   ○   ○

For much of 1997, news of the epic disaster film *Titanic* had dominated the motion-picture industry. Hollywood insiders saw its budget balloon to an immense $200 million, director James

Cameron give back his salary, and the original studio Paramount take on a partner (Twentieth Century–Fox) to spread the risk around. Industry observers began to predict a disaster of such gigantic proportions that it would make *Waterworld* (Kevin Costner's very expensive, greatly anticipated 1995 sci-fi epic, which bombed in theaters) look like a hangnail by comparison.

Once *Titanic* debuted, of course, it was a far different story. It went on to shatter box-office records worldwide (as of this writing, it's the top-grossing film of all time, with more than $600 million in North American receipts alone), win several Academy Awards, and lead the weekly box-office charts from its release in late 1997 through much of 1998.

Titanic wasn't the only 1997 entry that continued to show strength in early 1998. Both the Matt Damon/Ben Affleck hit, *Good Will Hunting,* and the Robert De Niro/Dustin Hoffman political satire, *Wag the Dog,* remained in the box-office top ten throughout the first weeks of 1998. In contrast, no new film released in the New Year had shown any kind of staying power at all.

Then came February 13, when *The Wedding Singer* opened in 2,281 theaters nationwide. The romantic comedy took in close to $22 million that Valentine's Day weekend, finishing second to *Titanic*'s $39 million gross.

It was immediately clear that New Line's marketing arm had done their job well: It wasn't just Adam's usual audience filling up theater seats for the new release. Sandler himself noticed the changing demographic when he snuck into a local movie house to check out the public's reaction to the vehicle. Used to seeing an audience full of baseball caps turned backward, this time, mixed in among his usual teen crowd, there were plenty of gray-haired and bald heads.

As significant as the movie's box-office success was its critical reception. Though the reviews on *The Wedding Singer* itself were still mixed, for the first time many critics found something appealing in Adam Sandler's screen persona.

Leonard Klaty, writing in *Variety*, decided, "Sandler, whose screen persona has been somewhat grating, is a revelation playing a character with innate decency. Unlike in past film work, you believe him as a romantic character and, even more important, that someone else would find him attractive. It is, quite simply, a breakthrough performance."

In the *Boston Globe*, critic Jay Carr judged, "So appealing is Sandler as a sweet Jewish boy from suburban New Jersey that it makes you wish he had stopped clobbering us with his lame attempts at comedy and gone this route a few years ago."

Virtually everyone associated with the movie received their fair share of positive feedback. Michael Rechstaffen (*Hollywood Reporter*) praised the "always splendid" Drew Barrymore; Roger Ebert (*Chicago Sun-Times*) singled out "the invaluable" Steve Buscemi; Bob Strauss (*Los Angeles Daily News*) cheered Frank Coraci's deft hand and "droll, affectionately askew" directorial eye; Carr of the *Boston Globe* found the cameos from *SNL* alumnus Jon Lovitz and rock star Billy Idol "as good-natured and almost as funny as Buscemi's."

Idol, who had to be talked into doing the part, now won big points at home for participating in the film. "I have an eight-year-old son, and he loves Adam, so now I'm a God for doing this. . . . Besides, I really love comedies, and I don't think there's enough of them. I don't think there are enough movies you can go to, be sitting next to your son, and be laughing at the same jokes," he told the online magazine *Hollywood.com* at the time of the film's release.

Mixed in among the largely favorable notices were some criticisms, of course, yet most reviewers seemed to go out of their way to find positive things to say about the feature. "[Sandler] looks ready to be funny throughout *The Wedding Singer,* [but] the screenplay doesn't always give him the chance," wrote the *New York Times*'s Janet Maslin. "Sandler and Barrymore keep digging for, and often strike, emotional honesty," added Bob Strauss of the *Los Angeles Daily News,* despite their being trapped in "hackneyed situations."

One prominent critic who gave the comedy an overall big "thumbs-down" was Roger Ebert of the *Chicago Sun-Times.* In bestowing the film with a rating of one star (out of a possible four), Ebert blasted not only the screenplay and its derivative, predictable plot, but, in particular, the leading man's performance.

"Sandler . . . always keeps something in reserve—his talent. It's like he's afraid of committing; he holds back so he can use the 'only kidding' defense," criticized Ebert. "Even at his most sincere, he sounds like he's doing stand-up, like he's mocking a character in a movie he saw last night."

There's a germ of truth in what Ebert says: In what is really only his second dramatic lead role (after *Bulletproof*), the comedian seems to play his "sensitive" scenes with a little less commitment than his "angry" ones. The most cathartic moment in the PG-13-rated movie, the one where what Robbie feels virtually jumps off the screen and hits the audience in the face (not to mention the heart) comes during his singing of "Love Stinks." Adam's scenes with Drew lack that special oncamera intensity— the two are so clearly made for each other from their first meeting that there's little fizz left in their romance by the time they do get together in the narrative.

Though the media initially focused on Adam's jump into romantic comedy, as the film continued to perform well at the box office (eventually taking in a total of $80 million in the United States alone), they found other things to write about. One person they zeroed in on was character actress Ellen Albertini Dow. The seventy-nine-year-old Dow played Adam's singing student, Rosie, who, at a party to celebrate her character's fiftieth wedding anniversary, performs a hilarious song/dance rendition of the Sugarhill Gang hit "Rapper's Delight." The rap dance/song scene was featured in ads for the movie, and articles about Dow—and her thirty-four-year career as a dance and mime teacher in California—appeared in publications nationwide. Her moment in the spotlight was similar to the one Bob Barker had enjoyed for *Happy Gilmore,* who reappeared in the wake of *The Wedding Singer*'s mega-success to complain—kiddingly—that Adam hadn't called him for a role in his new effort.

"No one ever heard of Adam Sandler," Barker told Kevin Thompson of the *Palm Beach* (Florida) *Post* in April 1999, "until I beat him up."

Another part of *The Wedding Singer*'s success story was its soundtrack album. "We wanted the best [songs] that we remembered," Producer Jack Giarraputo told *People* magazine, and they certainly got a great many 1980s favorites. The CD featured David Bowie's "China Girl," Culture Club's "Do You Really Want to Hurt Me?" and, of course, Billy Idol's "White Wedding." Also in the mix were two Adam-as-Robbie original compositions heard in the film—"Have You Written Anything Lately?" and "Somebody Kill Me."

The record shot into the *Billboard* charts, landing at #5 on the album charts: The original soundtrack's success inspired a second, and then a third volume of hits.

Everyone involved scored big with *The Wedding Singer*—no one more so than Adam, who barely a week after the film's opening, signed yet another picture deal with New Line Cinema. For a hefty $12.5 million salary, he agreed to do another movie with the studio—an as-yet-untitled comedy to be written by Tim Herlihy. The script, at that point, existed only as a one-line pitch: Adam as the reluctant successor to the family business, now being operated by his father, the devil. New Line paid an additional $2 million—slightly more than $100,000 per word—for the rights to that story, and Herlihy's services.

It should have been a time to celebrate. Yet for Adam, all the good news was leavened by sadness: Chris Farley's death the previous December continued to weigh heavily on his mind.

"It's hard for me to believe he's not with us anymore," Adam had told *E! Online* on the eve of *The Wedding Singer*'s opening. "*The Wedding Singer* will be the first time I've done a movie and Farley won't be calling me up the night it opens."

The Wedding Singer's success boosted Adam's profile even higher. Gossip columnists and supermarket tabloids began issuing frequent reports on what he was doing and with whom he was associating. He was at the premiere of Drew Barrymore's *Ever After* (1998) (true); the two of them were an item (false); he was back with actress Alicia Silverstone (false); he was going to host the MTV Movie Awards (false—though he had been asked and turned down the emceeing job, as had David Spade and Chris Tucker before Chris Rock finally accepted).

Adam did eventually appear at the MTV ceremonies on May 30, 1998, though, as a presenter and nominee: He and Drew

Barrymore were up for Best Kiss (against a strong field that included Joey Lauren Adams in her breakthrough role, from the movie *Chasing Amy*).

The evening would end with Adam taking home his second MTV Award: His good fortune, though, would again be tinged with sadness.

Comedian/actor Phil Hartman and Adam Sandler were never close the way Adam and the late Chris Farley had been. Hartman was from an earlier generation and he had a different style of humor. Where Adam and his *SNL* contemporaries, such as Farley, David Spade, and Rob Schneider, tended to create characters who were extensions of themselves, Hartman was a true mimic: one minute President Clinton, and the next spielmeister Ed McMahon. Hartman was able to blend into the background in any given situation. Approaching his fiftieth birthday, Phil was a good decade older than most of the comics around him at *SNL* as well, and was married to a beautiful wife (his third), with two young children and a plush home in the hills of Encino, California. Although Adam had turned his talents to movies after leaving *Saturday Night Live,* Phil Hartman had remained focused on television. The man Lorne Michaels had once called *SNL*'s glue was now a valuable cast member of two different series: FOX-TV's animated show *The Simpsons* and NBC's situation comedy *NewsRadio.* Hartman's name was one of the last anyone would expect to be associated with scandal.

Then, on May 28, 1998, two days before the MTV Awards, Hartman was found shot to death in his bed. Next to him, also dead, was his wife Brynn. Apparently, Brynn had fired at Phil several times while he slept. Then, after telling a friend what she had done, she lay down next to her husband and reportedly shot herself.

The tragic incident cast a pall over the entire MTV Awards ceremony. Both Mike Myers (who won an award for Best Villain) and Adam spoke of the loss: Myers dedicated his award to Hartman, calling him "one of the greatest character comedians ever." Myers also recalled Brynn as a "wonderful person and mother." Sandler, for his part, told the audience: "The Hartmans were great people. . . . It's very difficult to hear that news and also Farley being gone, it's a heavy-duty year."

Indeed, 1998 had been a roller-coaster ride for Adam—and the year was barely half over.

As it developed, the ride was just beginning.

CHAPTER 11

big bucks

"The weekend Waterboy *[1998] was released is my favorite*

moment since being in this business.

You couldn't go anywhere without people talking about it."

ACTOR/COMEDIAN ROB SCHNEIDER, 1999

A T ANY GIVEN POINT IN TIME, there are literally hundreds—
perhaps even thousands—of movie scripts floating around
Hollywood, bouncing back and forth between studio executives,
talent agencies, and actors. Some of these screenplays have been
optioned, which means someone (a studio, an actor, an indepen-
dent production company) has acquired the exclusive right, usually for a nominal fee and for a limited amount of time, to get the
movie made. Many more properties are simply out there, search-
ing for a home of some kind.

In either case, the odds are overwhelmingly against any one
of those screenplays being green-lighted (financed) by a major

studio. The caution is understandable—given that the average cost of making and releasing a film has ballooned into the tens of millions of dollars. Perhaps the most important factor in a studio's decision to make a movie is whether a bankable property— usually a hot actor—is attached to the project.

One script that had been lying around Hollywood for several years, which, in fact, had been optioned by Columbia Pictures, was titled *Guy Gets Kid,* by a writer named Steve Franks. Its premise involved a youngish adult forced by circumstance to adopt a child. Amy Pascal, who in early 1998 had become president of Columbia Pictures, sat in on an early screening of *The Wedding Singer* and was very impressed, in particular, by Adam's performance. At the same time Sid Ganis, a former Columbia executive who was just starting his own production company, brought Steve Franks's script to Pascal's attention. She thought *Guy Gets Kid* would be a perfect vehicle for Sandler, and spent weeks tracking down the star to discuss the project. Finally, she located him in an Atlantic City casino where he was playing slots with his dad. She quickly set up a meeting with Adam to discuss Franks's script. The result was not exactly what Pascal had anticipated.

"Adam said, 'I'm not gonna do it,'" Pascal recalled to *Entertainment Weekly* in June 1999. "And as he was walking out the door—and I was really devastated—he said, 'You know how we could make it work? We could make it work if we changed it so that I adopt the kid to get my girlfriend back.'"

Shifting the plot line—by making the relationship between the lead character and the young boy he adopts the catalyst for the hero's own decision to grow up—gave the film a far stronger story arc. It also allowed Adam to play the "loveable loser" prototype his fans had come to expect from him onscreen.

With the changes in the script agreed upon, Sandler began shooting the picture—now retitled *Big Daddy*—in fall 1998.

In the movie—the first Sandler picture to be shot and set in New York City—Adam is Sonny Koufax, a law school graduate who, having won a quarter-million dollars in a personal injury lawsuit (in which he was the plaintiff), has decided not to join the nine-to-five-job rat race. Instead, Sonny lives off the earnings from his settlement (he's invested his money in the stock market), with which he manages to pay rent on the loft he and his old law school buddy Kevin Gerrity share. Sonny also works one day a week as a bridge tollbooth collector.

Sonny's refusal to grow up and find real work irritates both his father and his girlfriend, Vanessa. Frustrated by his unrelentingly juvenile approach to life, Vanessa eventually lays down the law. Sonny must become an adult and join the real world, or they have *no* future together.

Koufax's pal Kevin, on the other hand, has decided to leap wholeheartedly into maturity by marrying his girlfriend, Corinne. Though she's a doctor now, Corinne helped pay her way through medical school by working as a waitress for Hooters—which amuses the immature Sonny. She, in turn, teases him right back about his loser lifestyle.

Corinne is at Sonny and Kevin's apartment the day a young boy is dropped off alone on their doorstep, accompanied only by a note. The message is from the boy's mother, living in upstate New York, and explains that the child—Julian—is actually Kevin's son. The mother never told Kevin about their offspring, but now she needs Kevin to take care of their son. Kevin is on his way to the Far East for a business trip . . . when Sonny has a brainstorm.

Sonny decides he'll take care of Julian to prove to Vanessa how mature he is. The plan, of course, backfires as she's already decided to leave him. Sonny and Julian, however, are stuck with each other until Kevin's return. Quickly, man and boy become pals. Precocious Julian even helps Sonny to meet a cute young woman he spots in the park—Layla Maloney, who turns out to be Corinne's sister.

When Child Services discovers Sonny is a fraud, they take Julian away and threaten to have Sonny jailed. By the film's fade-out, Kevin has returned from China and agrees to adopt his son. Meanwhile, Sonny and Layla have fallen in love, marry, and have a child of their own.

The production staff for *Big Daddy* was full of familiar names: Robert Simonds, Jack Giarraputo, Adam Sandler—and several new ones, most prominently, Sid Ganis, who had shown Columbia's Amy Pascal the original *Guy Gets Kid* script.

Returning to the Sandler fold as director was Dennis Dugan (who'd helmed 1996's *Happy Gilmore*) who was pleased to be on another Sandler project.

"I like the process that we have . . . it's very collegial," Dugan later told the *Hollywood Reporter*. "I'd work with Adam if he called and said, 'I've got an idea to dramatize the phone book.'"

This time around in Adam's new screen vehicle, there were no big-name co-leads. Veteran character actor Joseph Bologna (best known for his frequent costarring turns with his wife Rénee Taylor) played Adam's father, while Joey Lauren Adams (Sandler's rival back in June 1998 for the MTV Best Kiss Award) was attorney Layla Maloney. Actor/comedian Jon Stewart played Sonny's roommate Kevin Gerrity, and actress Leslie Mann (the real-life wife of Sandler's once college buddy Judd Apatow) took the role of Kevin's fiancée, Corinne.

For the pivotal role of Julian, the filmmakers chose young actor Cole Sprouse. Cole and his twin brother, Dylan, were show-business professionals—they'd worked in a toilet-paper commercial at six months old, and spent five years on the television show *Grace Under Fire* (1993–98). Six-year-old Cole had gone on the audition for *Big Daddy;* he and Adam had an immediate rapport. Dylan had originally been hired to help extend the shooting day (the number of hours child actors can work per day on a film set are stringently limited by law). When it became clear that each twin had his own particular strengths (Dylan, slightly more outgoing, did the action scenes; Cole handled the more introspective sequences), however, the two boys ended with fairly equal onscreen time.

As with all Sandler features, the set was calm, in fact, relaxed enough that the Sprouse twins felt free to behave like—well, like boys. "If they could fool around with us, they'd do it. They would pull on my beard all the time. . . . They would kid me about my gray hair," producer Sid Ganis later told the *Los Angeles Times*'s Saul Rubin, in a June 1999 interview. The boys and Sandler remained friends even after the shoot ended. Later that year, Adam sent them the pinball machine from "Sonny's" apartment as a Christmas gift.

The finished script for *Big Daddy* was filled with incidents modeled on the childhood experiences of both scripter Tim Herlihy and Sandler, as well as Herlihy's own trials as a new parent (his wife gave birth to a son halfway through the shoot). On the June 28, 1999, edition of the TV chat show *Live with Regis and Kathie Lee,* Adam revealed the real-life inspiration for the scene where his character, Sonny (dressed as a life-sized version of Julian's "Scuba Steve" doll), comes to the door to suggest Julian and his doll *both* hit the bathtub.

"I had a 'Diver Dan' doll I lost," Adam told Regis, relating an incident that had occurred while the Sandlers were still living in Brooklyn. "So my dad dressed up as Diver Dan's father and came to the front door. He said the doll was with him now, but 'thanks for watching him while he grew up.'"

Familiar faces and in-jokes are found throughout *Big Daddy*. Two other Sandlers—Jared and Jillian—make cameo appearances in the film, while the chameleon-like Allen Covert, long a part of Adam's extended family, takes a turn as one of Sonny's law school buddies. *Saturday Night Live* veteran Rob Schneider plays a deliveryman from the Famous Cozy Soup 'n' Burger (which was Adam and Tim Herlihy's onetime college hangout). Steve Buscemi is a homeless man who'd made some "bad choices" in high school, a reference to the character he'd played back in *Billy Madison*. Josh Mostel (Principal Anderson from the same 1995 Sandler comedy) is Mr. Brooks, the Social Services worker who takes Julian away from Sonny. Steven Brill—one of Adam's costars in 1989's *Going Overboard*—appears as Brooks's attorney Mr. Castellucci (a reference to Teddy Castellucci, Sandler's musical partner-in-crime from the "Goat Band" and *The Wedding Singer*, who also composed the original music used within *Big Daddy*).

There are others of Adam's in-crowd to be found in *Big Daddy*. The drunk at the end of the Blarney Stone bar (where Sonny and Julian go to watch the Jets play Monday Night Football) is named Mr. Herlihy: Mr. Herlihy (screenwriter Tim, that is) plays the Kangaroo in young Julian's "Kangaroo Song" video. Director Dennis Dugan—who had played Cybill Shepherd's twerpy husband in 1988 on the popular television series *Moonlighting*—jumps back in front of the camera for a turn as a reluctant trick-or-treat giver who Sonny helps to see the error of his ways.

The dark-haired waitress seen oncamera at the Blarney Stone was not a familiar face to Adam Sandler fans. Her brief appearance in *Big Daddy,* in fact, is actress/model Jacqueline Titone's feature film debut.

It wasn't the first time her name had been linked to Adam's, though: Supermarket tabloids and celebrity gossip sheets had been reporting the two of them as a romantic item for months.

As it happens, Jacqueline Titone proved to be the young woman with whom Adam Sandler had fallen in love.

○　　　○　　　○

"I'm finally a person who could be in a good relationship. When I was young, I was pretty stupid."

That is how Adam Sandler described himself in talking to writer Eric Layton of Los Angeles's *Entertainment Today* weekly publication back in February 1997. Given Adam's passion for living his life out of the public eye, few are privy to know exactly what mistakes he made when he was younger (though given the size and devotion of his female following from as far back as his early 1990s days at *SNL,* some educated guesses can be made). In November 1998, however, at the age of thirty-two, Adam Sandler was ready to settle down into a serious romantic relationship.

And Jackie Titone seemed to be it.

The two had first met at a party in Los Angeles. Adam had been instantly captivated. "I got hit hard," he told Regis Philbin in his June 1999 appearance on TV's *Live with Regis and Kathie Lee.* "Knocked over."

Adam asked Jackie out ("Wanna go to a baseball game?"), but she turned him down. Nonetheless, he kept asking.

The two eventually had their first date at a Houston's (a nationwide chain of barbecue restaurants) in Century City, California. For the record, Adam recalled Jackie had chicken for the main course. He learned that the tall, willowy Jackie was a model, a native of Lakeland, Florida, and was eight years his junior. ("When she was five years old and learning to read," Adam later joked with David Letterman on TV's *The Late Show,* "I was thirteen and learning to read").

In the entertainment business herself, Jackie could appreciate the demands Sandler's show business lifestyle required of him. She would have had to because, in the late fall of 1998, the two had little time together: Adam was involved in fifty-six of *Big Daddy*'s sixty days of shooting.

On Monday, November 8, though, they undoubtedly found time to celebrate. That was the day the box-office figures on *The Waterboy*'s opening weekend came in.

That was the day that Adam Sandler became a true Hollywood star.

The media likes things in fifteen-second sound bytes. Whether they're doing a story on a film, book, record, or what-have-you, they want to get in and get out quickly. They'd done that for every one of Adam's cinematic efforts, taking one particular moment from each film (Bob Barker's turn in *Happy Gilmore,* Adam's shower singing scene in *Bulletproof,* Ellen Albertini Dow's senior citizen rap dance in *The Wedding Singer,* and so forth) and highlighting it.

Media coverage on *The Waterboy*'s release, however, focused not on any one scene from the picture, nor a memorable guest star in the cast, or, for that matter, anything to do with the film's story. Media coverage this time around was all about the money: specifically, the $39.4 million the film took in on its opening weekend at 2,664 movie theaters.

That $39.4 million roughly equaled the combined opening-day grosses for *Billy Madison, Happy Gilmore,* and *The Wedding Singer.* It set a record for a fall (non-holiday) opening weekend: It fell just $1.4 million short of being Disney's all-time best opening film (an honor that belonged to 1994's animated feature, *The Lion King*).

"We were only mildly surprised," Phil Barlow of Disney/Touchstone told writer Jim Sullivan (*Boston Globe*) in an article that appeared on November 17, 1998. "We have a tracking service and we knew almost three weeks ahead of time that the storm was coming. But it's the level of success: We thought we had Mount Whitney; we ended up with Mount Everest."

Even if Disney was expecting healthy financial returns, the rest of the industry—for that matter, the entire country—was amazed.

"It's almost beyond description," Dan Marks of A. C. Nielsen (the ratings firm) told Rod Dreher of the *New York Post* (November 10, 1998). "He's the bankable guy now," agreed industry analyst Rich Ingrassia in the same newspaper report.

Everyone had their own theory for the explosive growth in Sandler's filmgoing audience. "I guess certain people thought they weren't supposed to see an Adam Sandler movie," director Frank Coraci suggested to *Entertainment Weekly* reporter Dave Karger the week after the hit picture debuted. "Thanks to *The Wedding Singer,* they're now aware that his movies aren't mean-spirited."

"There has always been this," CNN's movie analyst Martin Grove suggested to the *Boston Globe*'s Jim Sullivan. "Jerry Lewis. Charlie Chaplin, who was not initially about great art. Hollywood has always had a place in the mix for the clowns."

If Adam was flattered by those comparisons—or surprised by *The Waterboy*'s impressive financial success—he wasn't saying. On the set of *Big Daddy* it was pretty much business as usual.

"I'd say Adam's head swelled the least the day those first box-office grosses came in," actor Jon Stewart told Louis Hobson of the *Edmonton* (Alberta, Canada) *Sun.* "I think he was more happy for his friends than he was for himself."

Critical reaction to *The Waterboy* was (what else?) mixed . . . not that it mattered to anyone (as many critics themselves were now finally beginning to realize). "*Waterboy* Overflows with Repellent Humor," was the headline of Joan Anderman's critique in the *Boston Globe,* while Glenn Whipp's recap in the *Los Angeles Daily News* was titled "Sandler's *Waterboy* awash in laughter."

Writing in the *New York Times,* Janet Maslin suggested that "This escapist comedy is so cheerfully outlandish that it's hard to resist, and so good-hearted that it's genuinely endearing." On the other side of the coin—and continent—John Anderson of the *Los Angeles Times* wrote, "*The Waterboy* follows a leadenly predictable path."

As for the actors, costar Kathy Bates received her (usual) good notices. "Bates is a hoot as overbearing Mama Boucher and looks like she hasn't had this much fun in years," said the *Hollywood Reporter*'s Michael Rechstaffen. "Ms. Bates, decked out so colorfully that it looks as if the circus had come to town, is an utter hoot," added Maslin (*New York Times*).

Henry Winkler, in his first major motion picture role in years, also drew praise: "Winkler underplays nicely," wrote *Daily Variety*'s Glenn Lovell. "[He] plays the loveably hapless Coach Klein with cheerful restraint, even delicacy," said Andrew O'Hehir of the British film magazine *Sight & Sound*.

And as Vicki Vallencourt, Adam's tough-talking, motorcycle-riding, knife-wielding gal pal, Fairuza Balk gathered perhaps the most attention of all. "Firecracker Balk . . . finally gets to show her comedy chops," enthused Rechstaffen (*Hollywood Reporter*); she was "a casting coup" wrote Michael Ferraro (*Entertainment Today*); she was "sexy and funny," judged Lovell (*Daily Variety*).

As for the Waterboy himself . . .

The critics seemed to be coming around at last.

"You take less heat these days for saying you like Adam Sandler," *Rolling Stone*'s Fred Schruers pointed out, and a lot of reviewers stepped forward to agree.

"Sandler proves capable of occasional moments of grace to go with his trademark silliness," said Michael Ferraro (*Entertainment Today*); "Sandler keeps himself sweetly ridiculous while also managing to give his character some heart," wrote Janet Maslin (*New York Times*).

There were still those, of course, who felt differently.

Glenn Lovell (*Daily Variety*) judged, "As for Sandler, he remains an acquired (lack of) taste." Joan Anderman (*Boston*

Globe) hammered at "Sandler's screwed-up schoolboy antics" and the "cruel and offensive humor at the heart of [the film]." John Anderson (*Los Angeles Times*) concurred, adding that, of all the so-called "idiot comics" (his list included Pauly Shore, Chris Farley, and Jim Carrey), "[Sandler's] performances are the least performed, his characters the least realized."

(Left unmentioned by most reviewers was the fact that for this film Adam's character has his hair styled in almost a 1970s hillbilly kind of look, complete with sideburns.)

With the success of *The Waterboy,* in fact, there appeared in the press a whole new round of think pieces on the "dumbing-down" of American cinematic comedy.

"Sandler Happens" declared *Time* critic Richard Corliss, who then wrote in his November 23, 1998, article that "understanding Adam is a tough task for those hobbled by age or taste." (It was Corliss, incidentally, who'd called Adam "The Next Worst Thing" in 1996, at the time of *Bulletproof*'s release.) "Who are you calling Stupid?" asked the *Boston Globe,* in a piece that linked *The Waterboy* to a long tradition of such films as *National Lampoon's Animal House* (1978) and *National Lampoon's Vacation* (1983). The study in question featured thoughts from a sociology professor, a media critic, and another comedian on the reasons and speculations for Adam's rise to major success.

The story closed with a quote from Disney executive Phil Barlow, who wanted to put the entire debate in perspective.

"I believe also we sometimes overanalyze and undersimplify. This is a talented comedian people can identify with. He takes on the big guy and wins."

Some saw *The Waterboy* as a step backward in Sandler's development as an actor, that by falling back on a character that recreated the idiot mannerisms of his *SNL* Cajunman persona, he'd proven how limited his talent really was. Adam, too, reportedly, had problems with the film. According to information later published in *Premiere* magazine, Touchstone chairman Joe Roth had to convince Sandler not to pull out of the movie early in its development.

There is, however, another way to look at Adam's character and *The Waterboy* as a whole.

Although thirty-two-year-old Sandler is onscreen for virtually every scene of the movie's eighty-nine minutes, this PG-13-rated comedy is far more of an ensemble piece than any of his other releases so far. He's not necessarily the center of attention all the time—nor, with this talented cast, does he have to be.

It's very telling that the *The Waterboy* film clip that Adam took with him to all the TV talk shows featured Henry Winkler and Kathy Bates, not Adam. The promotional footage was of the scene where Coach Klein visits the Bouchers for dinner, hoping to talk Mama into letting Bobby play college football. In that sequence, Sandler allows the story line to dictate the comic focus—and that focus is Bates, not Adam. For all the talk about *The Waterboy* being a regression, it can also be argued that it's a step forward. Adam stays in character as quiet, respectful Bobby Boucher while Bates as Mama Boucher steals the screen time.

It's worth noting again, too, that at the heart of this screen comedy is the typical Sandler persona, the sympathetic underachiever who everyone could root for. The critics were at last picking up on this critical aspect of Adam's movie appeal.

"Something about Sandler" was the headline in the *Los Angeles Times,* for its article identifying Sandler's "underdog quality and core of vulnerability" as major reasons for his success.

The Waterboy did $25.2 million worth of business at the box office on its second weekend: It continued to draw well throughout the 1998 holiday season. By the time the film's theatrical run concluded in early 1999, it had grossed more than $160 million.

A final coda to Adam's new entertainment-business status: The October 30, 1998, edition of *Saturday Night Live* featured a skit parodying the long-running game show *Jeopardy.* One of the show's three contestants (played by cast member Jimmy Fallon) appeared wearing a flannel shirt and a baseball cap (turned backward on his head). The contestant spoke in non-sequiturs, he mumbled, he sang silly songs. This prompted the actor portraying the host in the skit to snarl, "I feel like I want to punch you." One suspects that more than a few people needed the identifying nametag Fallon's character was wearing (which read, simply: "Sandler") to figure out who the contestant was supposed to be. After *The Waterboy*'s success in November 1998 and thereafter, Fallon could have done the sketch without that nametag, and everyone would have known right away who he was lampooning.

Like it or not, Adam Sandler was now part of the American cultural landscape.

big daddy

"I know my life has changed. We write [movie parts]

for people and they actually say yes."

ADAM SANDLER, 1998

ACK IN 1994, WHEN ADAM SANDLER was still a cast member of NBC-TV's *Saturday Night Live,* he had no idea what to do with all the income he was accumulating. (Although Adam's salary at the time was not made public, several reports put his *SNL* castmate Chris Farley's salary for the following season at roughly $500,000. So, one can assume Sandler was pulling in somewhere close to that amount.)

Regarding the handling of his finances, Adam told writer Tom Green of *USA Today* at the time, "My brother . . . and my dad just take care of that. They explain it to me and five seconds later I tune out."

His comment really begs the question: What is Adam doing with all the money he is making now ($7 million for *The Waterboy,* $8 million for *Big Daddy,* $12.5 million for *Little Nicky*), as a bona fide Hollywood A-list star?

Of course, there was that Jaguar he bought his father.

And the pinball machine he gave the Sprouse twins for Christmas.

What else?

He got himself a black Cadillac.

His current girlfriend, actress Jackie Titone, as he would later tell TV gab-show host Regis Philbin, received "every other dress" she asked him for.

And then there was Sandler's Bel-Air mansion, which no doubt set him back a few of those millions. (Bel-Air is an enclave of expensive homes located just north of UCLA in Los Angeles, where those celebrities who actually desire their privacy, and can afford the real estate, live. Adam can definitely afford this pricey real estate.)

Yet his newfound wealth, and the accompanying indulgent lifestyle it could provide, seem to have changed the star scarcely at all.

Sandler, however, did get a bit of a wardrobe makeover in 1998. He excised the flannel shirt and the backward baseball cap that had been his standard in-public uniform throughout the 1990s. Paparazzi shots now typically catch Adam in a pair of baggy trousers and an oversized gray T-shirt with the word XXXL on it, or a warm-up suit, or an NYU sweatshirt ensemble. Sandler had cut his hair short for the *Big Daddy* shoot, and he now keeps it styled that way.

This look, however, is hardly haute couture.

"Glad to see you dressed up," TV's Jay Leno cracked during Adam's June 1999 appearance on *The Tonight Show*. What the talk show host did not mention, but the comedic movie star did reference on this television outing—as well as others—was that he had put on a little weight. The thirty-two-year-old Sandler was hardly fat, but he'd clearly filled out from his *SNL* days. (Sandler blamed "The damn White Castle [a New York city hamburger chain]" when explaining his fuller figure to David Letterman on a June 24, 1999, appearance on CBS-TV's *The Late Show.*)

Sandler the super celebrity appears to be comfortable with his new position in the show business hierarchy. More important than that, especially to his fans, he still seems real. Although he is definitely a movie star and making millions of dollars, he still comes across like the same old Adam Sandler to his public. He is someone with whom they can identify, someone who can speak to their concerns, someone who is willing, in fact, to make those concerns his own.

In November 1998, he refused to cross a picket line of striking workers to make an appearance on ABC-TV's *Good Morning America* to promote *The Waterboy*. Not even a personal plea from the network's news president David Westin could change his mind.

When organizers in his hometown of Manchester, New Hampshire, asked him in May 1999 to assist in publicizing the "Makin' It Happen Coalition for Resilient Youth" (a charitable organization designed to help children lead productive, drug-free lives), Adam put together a video with a new song, as well as a taped message urging kids to stay off drugs. In addition, Sandler continued to help his show-business friends, such as when he took time out to make a cameo appearance in buddy Norm Macdonald's first starring feature film, 1998's *Dirty Work*.

Unlike so many other celebrities who thrive in a rarified world all their own, Adam had, and has, his feet firmly planted in real life. Sandler knows how to be a regular person, certainly. Sometimes, in fact, it seems he has the act down a little too well.

"I was in New Hampshire with my family at a pizza place," Adam told *Twist* magazine in January 1999, *People Online Daily* reported. "The kid working there goes, 'Hey, you look like Adam Sandler.' I said, 'Yeah, I know.' He goes, 'What's your name?' I go, 'Adam Sandler.' And he goes, 'Whoa, that's a coincidence.'"

Bernie Brillstein, Adam's co-manager, told a story once of how comedian John Belushi, miffed at not being recognized at a bar in his Chicago hometown, stood up and bought everyone in the place drinks.

In comparison, thirty-three-year-old Adam Sandler—who, at the end of the twentieth century, stands at the top of the Hollywood celebrity heap in a way that John Belushi, even at the height of his success, never did—seemingly cares nothing about being recognized or even enjoying the extravagant perks of megastardom.

Being ultra-famous seems to hold absolutely no appeal or charm for Sandler.

○   ○   ○

Adam may not be keeping track of his status, but others certainly are.

For the year 1998, *People* magazine named Sandler one of "The 25 Most Intriguing People of the Year." *Entertainment*

Weekly placed him at number 4 on their "Entertainer of the Year" list. (Later in 1999, *Premiere* magazine published its list of the 100 most powerful people in Hollywood: Adam's ranking was at number 56, sandwiched between Michael Douglas and Meg Ryan.)

More importantly, Hollywood studios have stepped forward and recognized Sandler's A-list status. New Line Cinema renegotiated his deal for the upcoming movie *Little Nicky*, increasing his up-front salary from $12.5 million to $20 million. (This new film is now set for release in April 2000.) The studio also gave him a piece of the picture's coveted "back end" (the money the studio makes after recouping its production costs) as well. Long-time Sandler fan and New Line president Michael De Luca also signed Adam for yet another screen project—with subject matter "to be determined"—for an even larger, undisclosed amount of money.

"We have every intention of being a part of [Adam's] success for a long time to come," De Luca told the online entertainment magazine *Mr. Showbiz*.

Columbia Pictures was also intent on being in the Sandler business: Studio president Amy Pascal contracted Adam to develop (along with executive producer Jack Giarraputo) an animated musical feature. It would be the studio's first animated film. Columbia was banking on Adam (who would voice and serve as the basis for the picture's leading character) to help them break Disney's stronghold on feature animation.

"After our wonderful experience working with Adam on *Big Daddy*, everyone at Columbia is excited to be part of this new venture," Pascal enthused to *Daily Variety* in January 1999.

Theater owners, too, are intent on proving how much they love Adam. On January 21, 1999, the ShoWest Theater Directors

Association selected Sandler as their Comedy Star of the Year, making him the first actor ever to receive the award from both the ShoWest and ShowEast organizations. It was yet another indication within the movie industry of how valued a commodity Adam has become.

The newest member of the $20-million-dollar-per-movie club brought down the house with his acceptance speech at the awards ceremony two months later. "My name is Adam Sandler," he told the industry crowd gathered at Bally's Hotel in Las Vegas. "I'm not particularly smart. I'm not particularly talented. And yet, I am a multimillionaire." To increasing applause and laughter, the star went on to thank members of the organization for the part they'd played in his success.

Of course, he was being unduly modest. Perhaps he was even having a little fun before a room filled with not just theater owners, but also motion-picture reviewers, throwing back the criticisms that had been leveled at him over the years by the press. (One of the more interesting tidbits of information to emerge from the ShoWest convention was A. C. Nielsen company's research revealing that film reviews were important to only 9 percent of all moviegoers.)

It simply wasn't Adam's style to get up before a room full of people and discuss all the years of hard work that he'd invested to achieve his success. Nor would he have cared to reminisce over the countless times he'd stood perspiring before a handful of disinterested clubgoers, trying to get them to pay attention—let alone laugh at—his stand-up routines. He'd never bring up the endless all-nighters he'd pulled in his *SNL* office at 30 Rockefeller Center in Manhattan striving to get that new skit just right, or the endless rewrite sessions he and co-writer Tim Herlihy endured to hone *Big Daddy*'s screenplay closer to perfection.

But others were starting to trumpet Sandler's talent and strong work ethic.

"He makes it look easy, but Adam is the hardest worker you will ever meet," *Big Daddy* director Dennis Dugan told Steven Schaefer of the *Boston Herald* (June 20, 1999). "He works twenty-four hours a day; he writes, produces, co-edits."

"He is incredibly involved," concurred Columbia Pictures executive Amy Pascal in a June 18, 1999, interview with *Entertainment Weekly*.

"[Adam] knows what he wants," actor/comedian Rob Schneider told Schaefer. "He has fun, but he's there watching, hands on."

Sandler has a say in every decision related to his latest film: He is executive producer, screenwriter, and star. He is not, however, a dictator. "It's a team," director Dugan continued, "and we all have equal voices from the script on down to the final credits."

The press, in fact, has dubbed Adam and his core group of contributors "Team Sandler." Their goal, as Dugan sees it, is a simple one: "to tell a good story, and make it as funny as possible within the given circumstances."

The Team's movie sets are good places to work ("I was supposed to stay ten days, and I stayed ten weeks," Schneider recalled to Schaefer). Their leader is a good person to work for.

"[Adam's] a really fun guy," young actor Dylan Sprouse told Maria Speidel of *People* magazine (July 19, 1999) about working in *Big Daddy*. And he wasn't the only kid who liked Adam. On May 1, 1999, at the Nickelodeon Kids Choice Awards in Los Angeles, Sandler was named favorite Movie Actor (his *The Wedding Singer* costar Drew Barrymore was chosen as favorite Movie Actress).

Other concrete numbers testify to Adam's popularity: In the first week of *The Waterboy*'s video release (the seven-day span ending March 21, 1999), it shot to number 1 on the rental charts, adding another $8 million to the picture's total gross. All of which was good news for Columbia Pictures, who were banking on *Big Daddy* to be their big gun in the highly competitive summer box-office season.

Marketing campaigns made almost as much news as movies in the summer of 1999. George Lucas's mega-licensed, mega-blockbuster *Star Wars: Episode I—The Phantom Menace* opened the season: Artisan Entertainment's surprise smash *The Blair Witch Project* (fueled by an Internet marketing campaign that was the talk of the industry) closed it. And in between, there was *Big Daddy,* whose second round of outdoor advertising posters (following the all-type, non-illustrated ones which simply contained Adam's name, the film's title, and the picture's opening date) featured Adam and one of the young Sprouse twins peeing against the side of a building.

To say the ad campaign sparked controversy would be an understatement.

Big Daddy got its first big exposure in mid-June 1999, the week before it opened nationwide. Columbia Pictures hosted a full-scale Hollywood premiere at the Avco Theatre in Westwood, California—conveniently enough for Adam just around the corner from his Bel-Air home. After the screening, Columbia threw a party at the Barker Hangar (as the name suggests, a converted airplane storage facility) in Santa Monica to celebrate the comedy's imminent release. Seemingly, everyone who'd had a hand in the movie was in attendance: costars Joey Lauren Adams, Leslie Mann, Rob Schneider, Cole and Dylan Sprouse, and Kristy Swanson; director Dennis Dugan; executives Sid Ganis and Amy Pascal; as well as Adam, his parents (who he'd flown in from the East Coast for the event), and, of course, his girlfriend Jackie Titone. (According to *Hollywood Reporter* writer George Christy in his "The Great Life" column of June 25, 1999, Sandler aranged for Jackie to arrive at the festivities separately to protect her privacy.)

For the celebration, Columbia had transformed the hangar into a replica of the loft Adam and Jon Stewart's characters shared in *Big Daddy*. They decorated with sports pages and sports memorabilia, and served pizza, burgers, hot dogs, and so on, until the wee hours of the morning. Always the team player, Adam stayed until the festivities ended, signing autographs.

And that Friday—June 25—*Big Daddy* opened nationwide, bowing at 3,027 theaters. *Premiere* magazine, in its June 1999 issue previewing the summer blockbusters, had predicted a $120 million gross for the film.

Wrong by about a third.

By the beginning of fall 1999, *Big Daddy* was closing in on the $164 million mark: Its opening weekend gross of $41.2 million easily topped *The Waterboy*'s $39.4 million.

"It's been an amazing summer for all movies," producer Sid Ganis told Brian Fuson of the *Hollywood Reporter* the Monday after the opening box-office numbers were tabulated. "The [really] exciting thing for us is the broad range of the audience." Broad range is perhaps an understatement: Exit polls showed that 51 percent of *Big Daddy*'s audience was female.

That statistic is worth repeating: The weekend it opened, more women than men went to see the new Adam Sandler ("Mr. Teenage Male Audience") film.

Some of them, clearly, liked what they saw: 90 percent of that opening weekend audience rated the film as "excellent" or "very good."

Reviewer Janet Maslin of the *New York Times,* who'd been so complimentary to both *The Wedding Singer* (1998) and *The Waterboy* (1998), was disappointed. *Big Daddy,* she declared, consisted of "much less inventive material . . . [its] overabundance of nice-guy moments . . . gives the film tepid predictability instead of a cutting edge."

Kirk Honeycutt of the *Hollywood Reporter* thought differently. Compared to *The Waterboy,* he decided, "*Big Daddy* is Neil Simon." Wrong, said *People* magazine's Leah Rozen: "Compared to *The Waterboy, Big Daddy* is *Citizen Kane.*"

Many critics regarded the film as a calculated ploy on Adam's part to broaden his audience. "Sandler may play dumb, but he's no fool when it comes to shaping his movie image," said Susan Wloszczyna of *USA Today,* in giving the film a two-out-of-four-stars rating. "Designed to ring every demographic bell in the land," insisted David Ansen in *Newsweek.* "Calculated *Big Daddy* will please Sandler fans," headlined Jay Carr's piece in the *Boston Globe.*

Some reviewers saw *Big Daddy* no differently than any other Adam Sandler film. In *Time* magazine's June 21, 1999, review of the season's summer comedies, Richard Corliss labeled the movie "standard Sandler sociopathic humor." What was funny about the film, he went on to say, was "Sandler's 'acting' in the big emotional climax [and] the whim of the gods that made this meager talent a top star."

Meager talent? Wrong, declared Hal Hinson in the *Los Angeles New Times*, who judged Adam to be, "the most soulful—and the funniest—comic in the business." Robert Koehler of *Daily Variety*, though, sided with Corliss: "Sandler remains an extraordinarily limited actor who glides by on puppy-dog charm and charisma," he wrote.

This time around, the supporting cast of Adam's new screen vehicle received little special attention from the press, with the exception of Cole and Dylan Sprouse, who got their share of predictable "cute twins" stories in *People, Entertainment Weekly*, and so on. The spotlight remained firmly focused on Adam . . . even as the controversy surrounding the movie's poster of Adam and one of the Sprouse twins "watering" the side of a building (accompanied by the tag line: "Nature called. Look who answered") began to erupt.

"What was once a socially unacceptable act relegated only to skid row winos and the mentally ill is now, thanks to Hollywood marketing, being portrayed as funny, cute, and really cool," wrote Greg Crosby in the June 21, 1999, entertainment section of the *Los Angeles Times*. Readers were quick to respond, for the most part agreeing with Crosby. Here's a sampling of their responses:

"I wonder what went through the minds of [the] executives who approved this marketing strategy."

"Our homeowners association has been vigorously protesting *Big Daddy* billboards in our area."

"The PR types who are guilty [of this] campaign must be the people we remember from third grade who were willing to do anything to deface or destroy anything decent or beautiful."

"Few things in recent memory have been more discouraging/irritating than driving down the 405 freeway watching Adam Sandler and son pee on a giant billboard."

What did Adam have to say about all this?

As it turns out, not much. Looking more than a little uncomfortable when shown a copy of the offending ad on the TV talk show, *Live with Regis and Kathie Lee,* he claimed that, in the poster, his character is making a disapproving face toward young Julian. It's likely that, given his clout within the industry, he'd been at least consulted on the advertising campaign, and was having second thoughts about the image Columbia Pictures had chosen to publicize the comedy.

The ad inspired more than just controversy. The week following *Big Daddy*'s release, posters for Mike Myers's smash *Austin Powers: The Spy Who Shagged Me* were in circulation depicting that film's Dr. Evil and Mini-me in a similar bodily function pose to the one used to promote Adam's picture.

Though the *Big Daddy* ad campaign borders on tasteless, it must also be pointed out that the film itself bore the PG-13 rating label . . . which did indeed leave it up to parents whether to bring the impressionable minds everyone was so concerned with into the theater.

Ad promotion aside, *Big Daddy* not only confirmed Sandler's top-ranking status in the film business. It also marked a big step forward for Adam in other ways: specifically, his acting. In this movie, all the highlights were his. When, during the plot line, Social Services takes little Julian away, Adam's reactions—his desperate refusal to cry, his attempts to cheer Julian up, his promises to see the boy again soon—were the strongest work he'd ever done.

The film also featured a remarkable soundtrack, highlighted by Sheryl Crow's cover of the Guns 'n' Roses tune "Sweet Child of Mine." That song (which plays underneath footage of a disconsolate Sonny, shattered by the loss of Julian), in combination with Adam's restrained performance, made dialog unnecessary. Here, music and images are all that's necessary to create a hauntingly effective scene. The soundtrack also boasted a number of songs by Styx, the critically lambasted/popularly acclaimed 1980s rock group. Their decidedly negative real-life press coverage—and subsequent endorsement from the public—prompts within the movie Sonny's infamous "critics are cynical assholes" line.

But neither the soundtrack, nor Adam's strong work, nor even the controversy surrounding the marketing campaign could disguise the fact that *Big Daddy* was as predictable and inconsistent as many movie reviewers had charged.

Part of the problem lay in the casting: for all Joey Lauren Adams's skill and appeal as an actress, her character as written is too saccharine-sweet to be believed. A far better use of her megawatt smile and throaty voice might have been to cast her against type. Leslie Mann, on the other hand, is a delight as the ex-Hooters waitress. Despite the cutting nature of the onscreen insults between her and Adam's character, the genuine affection between the two of them is palpable—the filmmakers would have done well to play to that dynamic, rather than try to convince audiences that, within the plot, the two dislike each other.

A bigger creative problem, however, was the story itself. Giving the original plot premise a different twist—that is, making Sonny's motives for adopting Julian selfish ones—transformed a plot that had been done many times before (*Baby Boom*, 1987; *Three Men and a Baby*, 1987, and so on) into something fresh. Within *Big Daddy*, however, when Sonny's attempts to use Julian to affect a reconciliation with Vanessa fail, the movie returns to far too familiar, too predictable territory.

Virtually the entire cast (Adam, Leslie Mann, Jon Stewart, Joey Laurens Adams, Rob Schneider) did the TV talk-show circuit this time. Mann's appearance on NBC's *The Tonight Show* was a particular highlight. She told host Jay Leno that, in order for her to be believable as a Hooters girl, the producers had to "add" to her natural assets with a pair of fake breasts. Leslie then presented those to Leno in a cardboard box as a way of saying "thank-you" for being so nice to her a year ago when she'd made her talk-show debut on his late-night program.

Then came the evening's highlight. Leslie showed a video clip that her husband, Judd Apatow, had made of Adam back when the two of them were NYU dormmates in the mid-1980s.

"Adam would call [delicatessens] and pretend he was an old woman, who had eaten bad roast beef," Mann detailed to Leno, setting up the clip for the audience. "So he'd try to get them to give him a free sandwich next time he came in."

The clip—which shows Adam sitting in bed in his pajamas, talking in his "old Jewish grandma voice"—had the studio audience in stitches. It also provided a very concrete demonstration to viewers nationwide of just how long Adam had been in show business. Watching the young Sandler in the video, contrasting him with the thirty-two-year-old man in *Big Daddy*, it was also obvious—perhaps for the first time—that "Billy Madison" was indeed growing up.

And—the gossip grapevine had it—getting married. Rumors of Adam and Jackie Titone's engagement had begun appearing in the press a few months before the premiere of *Big Daddy*. The *National Enquirer* went so far as to track down Adam's dad in Florida, phoning to offer him both congratulations and the gift of a houseplant.

"I have no comment," Stanley Sandler told them, "but I'll take the plant."

Adam and his publicist both categorically denied the matrimonial rumor, not once but several times. About the only thing that could be said for sure was that Adam and Jackie were living together as a couple, and that their relationship was serious. Some also speculated that working with the Sprouse twins in *Big Daddy* had set Adam to thinking about, at long last, settling down and having a family of his own.

"I've watched Adam around children," actress Leslie Mann told writer Louis Hobson of the *Calgary* (Alberta, Canada) *Sun* on June 20, 1999. "He loves them and they love him. . . . I think he'd make a great dad."

Growing older was on Adam's mind. When Diane Sawyer asked him on ABC-TV's *Good Morning America* what had changed the most for him after all his success, he replied "my waist size."

Back in February 1998, Adam had told Eric Layton of *Entertainment Today* that he was planning on someday doing a movie from behind the camera, in a producing/directing capacity.

"I'm sure it's gonna happen," he'd said at the time. "The biggest reason is, I can start eating as much as I want. I'm tired of having to worry about my chins."

In July 1999, Adam took his first step in that direction, forming a new production company: Happy Madison films. Almost immediately, the company announced its first screen project: *Deuce Bigalow: Male Gigolo.*

To be financed by Disney/Touchstone and produced by Sid Ganis and Barry Bernardi (Adam and Jack Giarraputo would be executive producers), the $15 million picture would give Rob Schneider his first feature film starring role.

"[I play] a guy who cleans fish tanks for a living," Schneider told Conan O'Brien of NBC-TV's *Late Night* in June 1999. "[I'm] taking care of the fish tanks of this gigolo and I completely trash the place so I have to go out with these women clients of his to make enough money to fix the place up."

Marlo Thomas (TV's *That Girl* of 1967–71), Gail O'Grady (best known for her role in the TV series *N.Y.P.D. Blue*, 1993–present), and veteran film and television actor William Forsythe (who played notorious gangster Al Capone in the 1992–94 revival of TV's classic series, *The Untouchables*) were brought on board to costar with Schneider. Oded Fehr (*The Mummy*), Eddie Griffin, and Arija Bareikis filled out the cast, while Adam himself was scheduled to make a cameo appearance. (The film is currently scheduled for a December 3, *1999* release.) Auspiciously enough, the film (which producer Ganis promised would be as raunchy as possible and still hold on to its PG-13 rating) started shooting on July 6, 1999, just as *Big Daddy* hit the $100 million mark. A good sign for Adam, who, having conquered the Hollywood universe as an actor, was moving on to other industry fronts.

And, as always, making sure to take "Team Sandler" with him.

CHAPTER 13

the last word

"When I see my name [in print], I run away. I don't know

what's being said, or what lies are being spread.

I heard I was dead [once]. I got a lot of calls."

ADAM SANDLER, 1997

WHAT DO WE KNOW, ULTIMATELY, about today's thirtysomething Adam Sandler?

As reported in the *Globe* (November 24, 1998) for "10 Fun Facts You Didn't Know about Adam Sandler," the comedian enjoys talking on the phone (his long distance bill sometimes approaches $700 a month).

He likes sports. When the New York Knicks were making their improbable run into the 1999 NBA finals, Adam flew back and forth between New York and Los Angeles to catch his beloved basketball team in action at Madison Square Garden.

He is not, in the words of *People* magazine (who put him on their 1999 list of Worst Dressed People), a "big dresser." "He's doing the 'I'm a frat boy and I just got out of college routine,'" suggested fashion expert Pamela Keogh.

He values his privacy deeply.

As successful as Sandler is today, he insists—as he told *E! Online* in 1999—that "I still get very scared when I step in front of a live audience." He also informed the same Internet Web site that he is *not* a good audience for himself: "I don't laugh at me. I used to. I used to get the giggles when I'd see myself. But now, I see myself onscreen, and I sure don't laugh. Seeing [Chris] Farley always made me laugh."

When his mother can't sleep, according to the *Globe,* she calls Adam, and he sings her "Maria" from the musical *West Side Story* until he hears her snoring.

He's incredibly loyal to his friends.

He doesn't worry about selecting the "right" screen roles. As he told *E! Online* in 1999, "I don't think people say, 'I wonder what Adam's next movie is going to be.' My movies must kind of sneak up on you. I don't have to worry too much about what everybody is going to say. Anyway, I really don't pay attention to what the world says about my movies. I just care about what my buddies think."

And Sandler does not care to talk to the press. Why?

"He's basically quite shy," *Big Daddy* (1999) costar Leslie Mann told Louis Hobson of the *Calgary* (Alberta, Canada*) Sun* in June 1999.

"Adam doesn't need to do interviews. Everybody knows who he is," actor/comedian Rob Schneider said, in the same article. "*I* [emphasis added] need to do interviews."

"I don't think he feels as comfortable doing print interviews as he does TV," director (*Happy Gilmore, Big Daddy*) Dennis Dugan told journalist Louis Hobson of the *Calgary Sun.*

Possibly this is so. It's also true, however, that it was the same critics who had savaged Adam and his work on more than one occasion who were now banging down his door for a quote. While he considers whether to take time out of his schedule to help them out, one thing that no doubt factors into his thinking has to be how little they'd tried to understand his creative output over the years.

"Adam is often dismissed by people who aren't necessarily mean-spirited but just lazy," according to Bill Thompson, film critic for the Charleston, South Carolina, *Post and Courier.* "They don't even try to understand the reasons for his success."

As Sandler's popularity has grown, those misunderstandings have reached a whole new level. On July 7, 1999, NBC-TV's prime-time newsmagazine show, *Dateline,* aired a piece titled "Teen Idol," a segment devoted to figuring out the secret to Adam Sandler's enormous show-business success.

On-air reporter Josh Mankiewicz pointed to the increased purchasing power of teenagers (they buy 37 percent of all movie tickets, according to figures presented on the program), the relatively low cost of producing "gross-out" screen comedies, and then he touched, ever-so-briefly (two sentences), on Sandler's talent for relating to today's powerful teen audience.

Dateline's Mankiewicz, as had so many other critics over the years, ducked the hard questions. If making gross-out teen movies is such a box-office slam dunk, why doesn't everyone do it successfully? Why has Adam Sandler become a star, and Pauly Shore (whose mid-1990s box-office clout was roughly equivalent to Sandler's) evolved into a comedy punchline? The piece also ignored some telling facts: 47 percent of the opening night audience for 1998's *The Waterboy* was female. As previously cited, that number jumped to 51 percent for 1999's *Big Daddy*. *Dateline* appeared unwilling to give Adam—and Team Sandler—credit for anything other than perfecting the teen gross-out film genre.

Keener observers are starting to realize that there is something more at the core of each of Adam's movies than a few bodily function jokes.

"He takes pains to make sure his stories have a degree of heart," New Line Cinema's president Michael De Luca told the *New York Times* in November 1998.

"He has a link to the psyche of an awful lot of people," agreed executive Phil Barlow of Touchstone/Disney in the same article.

"[Adam] is one of those special performers who is able to do exactly what he wants, no matter if it's as wacky as *The Waterboy*, and still let everyone see the heart in him," director Dennis Dugan said to the *Boston Globe*'s Stephen Schaefer just prior to *Big Daddy*'s release.

Adam has not cared to debate his artistic choices with the media. What they think apparently doesn't matter to him.

"I wish I could get him to talk about himself sometime," his manager Sandy Wernick told *Newsweek* in the fall of 1998. "It's not important to him. What's important to him is making his movies and having all his buddies around him."

What was most emphatically not crucial for Adam was what the movie critics had to say. One suspects, however, that feedback from his peers has touched him a little more deeply—particularly when it comes from one of his childhood idols.

○   ○   ○

"I'd enjoy driving in smoggy L.A. with my windows open more than watching *The Waterboy.* . . . Adam Sandler doesn't make me laugh."

That quote comes from an interview Bill Murray did with the *New York Times Sunday Magazine* published in January 1999. This was actor Bill Murray, whose film *Caddyshack* (1980) was Adam's comic touchstone. This *Saturday Night Live* veteran was referenced by Adam once as, "There's nothing better than when Bill comes by and says 'Hey, that thing you did was funny.'"

That's Bill Murray, going out of his way to slam Adam's work. And Murray wasn't the only *Saturday Night Live* veteran who found Sandler's success disturbing.

On Sunday, June 6, 1999, Loew's Santa Monica Beach Hotel in California played host to a symposium entitled "Words into Pictures," where a panel of comedy screenwriters talked about what was funny—and what was *not*. Onstage were comedians Albert Brooks, Janeane Garofalo, Harry Shearer, and Norm Macdonald, as well as several other industry veterans.

A chance mention of Adam Sandler's name turned the discussion into a debate on his movies. Brooks—who had produced a number of short films for *SNL* during the 1970s Not Ready for Prime Time years, and had since gone on to write and direct several notable screen comedies, including *Lost in America* (1985), *Mother* (1996), and *The Muse* (1999)—attacked much of Adam's humor as mean-spirited.

"And just because it makes a whole lot of people laugh doesn't mean it's great," added Garofalo.

Brooks went on to compare Adam to a disease that the country seemed hooked on. "Let's do what else America likes. How about cancer? They all seem to get that. Must be good!"

Part of what Brooks (and Garofalo) were saying sounded like sour grapes. The educated guess here is that if you added up the box-office receipts for all of Brooks's pictures, you'd get a total roughly equivalent to *Big Daddy*'s opening weekend gross.

Part of what they were saying felt like some bizarre attempt to assign one kind of humor (as seen in their films) a higher value than another (as seen in Adam's screen comedies). That notion, *Saturday Night Live* creator/executive producer Lorne Michaels pointed out in a 1998 defense of Adam's movies to Richard Corliss of *Time,* made as much sense as analyzing the nutritional value of a candy bar.

"Everybody knows what a Snickers is and why you like it. To deconstruct it, to point out that it only has peanuts and chocolate, is to take all the fun out of eating it."

But there was a valid point hidden in Albert Brooks's stinging critique.

"Adam Sandler on *Saturday Night Live* has made me laugh lots and lots and lots of times," Brooks told the audience. "[But] there's something about [Hollywood] that is very difficult to master. . . . Sometimes the structure of the movie becomes safer than the comedian wants to be . . . or more mainstream or whatever it is that you need to be to get $60 million to make a movie."

(It should be noted that the Albert Brooks attacking Adam Sandler's films here is the same Albert Brooks quoted in a July 11, 1999, *Los Angeles Times* article on the new wave of low-brow comedies as saying, "The beauty of these [films] is that you don't have to see them to hate them." One wonders if Brooks has, indeed, seen many or any Adam Sandler movies.)

Big Daddy was the best example of that safeness to which Brooks pointed. Its script, as mentioned earlier, was too highly predictable. It seems foolish to suggest that someone in Hollywood forced Adam to make it that way. After all, he's the one who gave the original story line a much-needed twist. It seems equally silly to imply that Adam and Tim Herlihy, in rewriting the script, consciously included a particular scene, or character, to draw in a target demographic.

That's not the way that Adam Sandler thinks—and/or talks.

That is, however, the language that studio executives use. And therein, as veteran comedian Harry Shearer (*SNL, This Is Spinal Tap, The Simpsons*) points out, lies the real problem with the most recent wave of "low-brow" comedies.

"It's wrong to say our culture is being run by twelve-year-old boys," Shearer stated in a July 11, 1999, piece for the *Los Angeles Times*. "It's being run by the guys in their forties who are pandering to the tastes of twelve-year-olds. Even twelve-year-olds have broader tastes."

Business people trying to find a formula for successful art will inevitably fail, because there is no formula. Audiences can tell the difference between something that comes from the heart and a studio creation, between reality and artifice. That's why Adam Sandler's movies reach them, and David Spade's (whose eyebrow seems to always be arched just a little bit, as if to say to the audience, "Well, this is pretty funny, isn't it?") fall a bit flat.

It's why the 1995 wholesale turnover at *SNL* mandated by NBC executives Warren Littlefield and Don Ohlmeyer had no noticeable effect on improving the quality and/or popularity of that show.

You can't legislate laughter. You can, however, fine-tune your craft. It's worth noting that the Sandler film that had far and away the most positive critical response was *The Wedding Singer*, whose script had been gone over not just by Adam and Tim Herlihy, but by Carrie Fisher and Judd Apatow as well. It would be interesting to see Adam apply his own mainstream comic sensibility (and his considerable skills as a performer) to a different kind of project altogether . . . perhaps, say, an Albert Brooks film.

What's up next professionally for Adam Sandler?

The Rob Schneider vehicle *Deuce Bigalow: Male Gigolo*, executive produced by Adam and in which he plays a cameo role, is before the cameras, set to be released in December 1999. Shooting on Sandler's next starring screen vehicle, *Little Nicky*, was set to start in November 1999, with Adam's old friend Steven Brill directing. (Brill, apart from his work as an actor in *Going Overboard*, *The Wedding Singer*, and *Big Daddy*, is best known as the writer of Disney's *Mighty Ducks* movie series.) Harvey Keitel (*Get Shorty*, *The Piano*) would play Adam's father, Satan, with Patricia Arquette (*True Romance*, *Stigmata*) as Sandler's love interest and Rhys Ifans (*Notting Hill*) as his brother. And at long last, Adam would be working with one of his major childhood idols, Rodney Dangerfield, who had been added to the *Little Nicky* cast.

Stanley Sandler must be proud.

And speaking of Adam's dad . . .

Stan and Judy's Kid, the comedian's fourth CD, was released on September 21, 1999. Produced again by Sandler and music industry veteran Brooks Arthur, the Warner Bros. album features a mixture of songs and skits, new characters, and familiar themes. Music industry legend Ray Ellis (who has written, produced, and recorded songs for Billie Holiday, Barbra Streisand, Johnny Mathis, Lena Horne, Tony Bennett, and Paul Anka, among others) made contributions to the album, as did a number of Frank Sinatra's old sidemen.

New skits on the record involve "The Peeper" and "The Cool Guy." New musical tracks include "The Chanukah Song 2" and "7 Foot Man," a Latin-tinged number that acoustic-guitar-wielding Adam performed on the September 22, 1999, edition of CBS-TV's *Late Show*. Sandler may also do a limited series of United States tour stops to support his latest album.

Beyond traditional concert appearances, Adam continues to reach out to his audience in new ways. For example, on September 3, 1999, he became the very first major motion-picture star to debut a new film on the Internet: *The Peeper,* a six-minute animated item based on the skit from *Stan and Judy's Kid.*

"The on-line community has always been supportive of me, and I wanted to give them something in return," Adam told *USA Today*'s Claudia Puig on August 24, 1999. "I wanted to give the ability to watch it whenever they got the urge. Long live the Web!"

Over the 1999 Labor Day weekend, the short subject, written by Adam and Allen Covert, drew over one million Internet viewers to Adam's own Web site (www.adamsandler.com) as well as to several Warner Bros. sites (see appendix C for a list of Sandler-related Web sites). "'Peeper' could serve as a model for the future of mainstream programming in the online world," declared Jim Moloshok, president of Warner Bros. Online, in a September 8, 1999, *Daily Variety* piece.

Meanwhile, back in the real world, Adam joined in the NBC-TV celebration for *SNL*'s 25th anniversary. On September 26, 1999, in front of a studio audience consisting of virtually every

SNL cast member and guest host in the show's quarter-century on the air, Sandler spoke lines fed to him by (in turn) former head writer/producer Jim Downey, former writer Robert Smigel, and current producer Tim Herlihy, which was intended to demonstrate how dependent the cast was on its writing staff.

Though that appearance was the first time in almost five years that Adam and his old *SNL* buddies had been together, Sandler and Tim Herlihy are in constant communication with each other, faxing script ideas back and forth across the continent (Herlihy lives in Connecticut; Adam spends most of his time in Bel-Air). As for the rest of Team Sandler, Frank Coraci is directing the big-screen version of *Charlie's Angels*. As previously mentioned, Jack Giarraputo is executive producing both *Deuce* and Adam's animated movie venture. And it wouldn't be surprising to see comedian/actor Allen Covert pop up somewhere in the previously mentioned movies.

Then there's Jackie Titone—who, the media keeps on insisting, is about to become Mrs. Adam Sandler. Adam and his representatives continue to assert otherwise.

Odds are, at some point in the not-too-distant future, Adam Sandler will marry and have children. Then, they will be two more real-life milestones that he'll no doubt incorporate into his screen work, the same way he has used the outsider/class-clown/loveable-loser periods of his life as film fodder. If there's one thing that's true about Adam Sandler, it's that the characters he plays in his movies are, at their core, simply variations of himself—a self that is, as director Dennis Dugan told journalist Stephen Schaefer, "a really decent human being."

Again, this puts Adam squarely in the line of a long Hollywood tradition of actors who have been able to project their offscreen persona onto their big-screen image (John Wayne, Henry Fonda, Jimmy Stewart, and others) and have people relate to it. How Adam's audience continues to relate to him, particularly as he grows older, will ultimately determine his long-term staying power.

One comedian whose long-term staying power (and career) has some interesting parallels to Adam's is Jerry Lewis. In his heyday during the late 1950s and early 1960s, Lewis was not only one of the biggest film stars in the world (his 1959 deal with Paramount Pictures for $10 million plus 60 percent of the profits for fourteen films set an industry record), but also a highly successful recording star (his *Rock-A-Bye Your Baby with a Dixie Melody* Decca record album sold close to four million copies), and an award-winning director (an eight-time Best Director of the Year winner in Europe).

Though Sandler rarely refers to Jerry Lewis as a major influence, the two clearly have much in common. As the online entertainment magazine *Mr. Showbiz* pointed out, "Lewis was the first entertainer to release his Inner Child. . . . His hyperactive, goofy little-boy routine was hysterically funny to fifties audiences." Lewis's popularity, like that of Sandler, went hand-in-hand with much adverse critical comment, none of which had any effect whatsoever on his ability to make successful films behind, as well as in front of, the camera and to have a long and productive career.

As for what else the future holds for Adam Sandler . . .

"I don't have a plan," Adam told writer Lewis Beale of the *New York Daily News* back in 1994, "but I don't ever want to get to the point where people are sick of me."

Half a dozen years later (though some critics continue to call for his head on a plate), Adam Sandler remains someone who the

American public lines up to see. Someday, of course, people will no doubt tire of him. The generational cycle will turn, and tomorrow's teens will find another comic hero to shoot to the top of the movie box-office charts.

When that day comes, Adam may well pick up *Time* magazine to find angry critics condemning those new comics and praising the good old days when screen clowns like Sandler and Jim Carrey ruled America's megaplexes.

That day, however, remains far in the future. For now, Adam continues to move from project to project, from media to media, keeping his own comic muse fresh and invigorated.

Above all, millions of people across the country continue to enjoy the ride.

filmography (and television)

FEATURE FILMS

Going Overboard (TriMark, 1989) 87 minutes, R-rated.
Credits: Producer: Randolf L. Turrow; Director: Valerie Breiman;
Screenplay: Valerie Breiman.

Cast: Adam Sandler (Shecky Moskowitz); Burt Young (General
Noriega); Billy Zane (King Neptune); Milton Berle (Himself);
Lisa Collins Zane (Miss Australia); Tom Hodges (Bob); Billy Bob
Thornton (Dave); Allen Covert (Bartender); Peter Berg (Bit).

Shakes the Clown (I.R.S. Releasing, 1991) 83 minutes, R-rated.
Credits: Producers: Paul Colichman and Ann Luly; Director: Bob
Goldthwait; Screenplay: Bob Goldthwait.

Cast: Bob Goldthwait (Shakes the Clown); Julie Brown (Judy); Bruce
Baum (Ty the Rodeo Clown); Steve Bean (Beaten Mime in Park);
Blake Clark (Stenchy the Clown); Paul Dooley (Owen Cheese);
Robin Williams (Mime Jerry/Marty Fromage); Kathy Griffin
(Lucy); Adam Sandler (Dink the Clown); Florence Henderson (The
Unknown Woman); La Wanda Page (Female Clown Barfly).

Coneheads (Paramount, 1993) 88 minutes, PG-rated.
Credits: Producer: Lorne Michaels; Director: Steve Barron; Screenplay:
Dan Aykroyd, Tom Davis, Bonnie Turner, and Terry Turner.

Cast: Dan Aykroyd (Beldar Conehead); Jane Curtin (Prymaat Conehead); Michael McKean (Seedling); Michelle Burke (Conjab "Connie" Conehead); David Spade (Eli Turnbull); Chris Farley (Ronnie); Jason Alexander (Larry Farber); Michael Richards (Motel Clerk); Sinbad (Otto); Phil Hartman (Marlax); Adam Sandler (Carmine); Parker Posey (Stephanie); Kevin Nealon (Senator); Ellen DeGeneres (Coach); Laraine Newman (Laarta); Jon Lovitz (Dentist); Tom Arnold (Golfer); Drew Carey (Taxi Passenger).

Airheads (Twentieth Century–Fox, 1994)
91 minutes, PG-13-rated.

Credits: Producers: Robert Simonds and Mark Burg; Director: Michael Lehmann; Screenplay: Rich Wilkes.

Cast: Brendan Fraser (Chazz Darby); Steve Buscemi (Rex); Adam Sandler (Pip); Chris Farley (Wilson); Michael McKean (Milo); Judd Nelson (Jimmie Wing); Ernie Hudson (O'Malley); Amy Locane (Kayla); Nina Siemaszko (Suzzi); David Arquette (Carter); Michael Richards (Doug Beech); Joe Mantegna (Ian the Shark); Harold Ramis (Chris Moore); Allen Covert (Cop); Mike Judge (Radio Voice of Beavis and Butt-Head).

Mixed Nuts (TriStar, 1994) 97 minutes, PG-13-rated.
Credits: Producers: Paul Junger Witt, Tony Thomas, and Joseph Hartwick; Director: Nora Ephron; Screenplay: Delia Ephron and Nora Ephron.

Cast: Steve Martin (Philip); Madeline Kahn (Blanche Munchnik); Robert Klein (Mr. Lobel); Anthony LaPaglia (Felix); Juliette Lewis (Gracie Barzini); Rob Reiner (Dr. Kinsky); Adam Sandler (Louie); Liev Schreiber (Chris); Rita Wilson (Catherine O'Shaughnessy); Parker Posey and Jon Stewart (Rollerbladers); Joely Fisher (Susan); Garry Shandling (Stanley Tannenbaum); Steven Wright (Man at

Pay Phone); Haley Joel Osment (Little Boy); Michael Badalucco (AAA Driver).

Billy Madison (Universal, 1995) 88 minutes, PG-13-rated.
Credits: Producer: Robert Simonds; Director: Tamra Davis; Screenplay: Tim Herlihy and Adam Sandler.
Cast: Adam Sandler (Billy Madison); Darren McGavin (Brian Madison); Bridgette Wilson (Veronica Vaughan); Bradley Whitford (Eric Gordon); Josh Mostel (Max Anderson); Norm Macdonald (Frank); Mark Beltzman (Jack); Theresa Merritt (Juanita); Dina Platias (Miss Lippy); Diane Douglas (Nurse); Tim Herlihy and Frank Nakashima (Architects); Chris Farley and Steve Buscemi (Bits).

Happy Gilmore (Universal, 1996) 92 minutes, PG-13-rated.
Credits: Producer: Robert Simonds; Director: Dennis Dugan; Screenplay: Tim Herlihy and Adam Sandler.
Cast: Adam Sandler (Happy Gilmore); Christopher McDonald (Shooter McGavin); Carl Weathers (Chubbs Peterson); Julie Bowen (Virginia Venit); Frances Bay (Grandma); Allen Covert (Otto); Robert Smigel (IRS Agent); Bob Barker (Himself); Richard Kiel (Mr. Larson); Kevin Nealon (Potter); Ken Camroux (Coach); Ben Stiller (Nursing Home Attendant); Dennis Dugan (Doug Thompson).

Bulletproof (Universal, 1996) 85 minutes, R-rated.
Credits: Producer: Robert Simonds; Director: Ernest Dickerson; Story: Joe Gayton; Screenplay: Joe Gayton and Lewis Colick.
Cast: Damon Wayans (Rock Keats); Adam Sandler (Archie Moses); James Caan (Frank Colton); Kristen Wilson (Traci Flynn); Jeep Swenson (Bledsoe); James Farentino (Captain Jensen); Larry McCoy (Detective Sulliman); Allen Covert (Detective Jones);

Bill Nunn (Finch); Mark Roberts (Charles); Mark Cassella (Disneyland Cop).

The Wedding Singer (New Line Cinema, 1998)
96 minutes, PG-13-rated.

Credits: Producers: Brad Grey and Robert Simonds; Director: Frank Coraci; Screenplay: Tim Herlihy.

Cast: Adam Sandler (Robbie Hart); Drew Barrymore (Julia Sullivan); Christine Taylor (Holly); Allen Covert (Sammy); Angela Featherstone (Linda); Matthew Glave (Glenn Gulia); Alexis Arquette (George); Frank Sivero (Andy); Christina Pickles (Angie Sullivan); Ellen Albertini Dow (Rosie); Jodi Thelen (Kate); Steve Buscemi (Drunken Best Man); Patrick McTavish (Tyler); Billy Idol (Himself); Kevin Nealon (Mr. Simms); Todd Hurst (Drunken Teenager); Earl Carroll (Justice of the Peace); Steven Brill (Glenn's Buddy); Jon Lovitz (Jimmy Moore); Tim Herlihy (Rudy the Bartender); Josh Oppenheimer (Member of David's Band), Teddy Castellucci (Member of Robbie Hart's Band).

The Waterboy (Touchstone, 1998) 89 minutes, PG-13-rated.

Credits: Producers: Jack Giarraputo and Robert Simonds; Director: Frank Coraci; Screenplay: Tim Herlihy and Adam Sandler.

Cast: Adam Sandler (Bobby Boucher); Henry Winkler (Coach Klein); Kathy Bates (Mama Boucher); Fairuza Balk (Vicki Vallencourt); Jerry Reed (Red Beaulieu); Larry Gilliard Jr. (Derek Wallace); Blake Clark (Farmer Fran); Peter Dante (Gee Grenouille); Jonathan Loughran (Lyle Robideaux); Al Whiting (Casey Bugge); Clint Howard (Paco); Allen Covert (Walter); Rob Schneider (Townie); Frank Coraci (Roberto); John Farley (Tony Dodd); Kevin Farley (Jim Simonds); Paul "The Giant" Wright (Captain Insano); Dave Wagner (Announcer); Mattie Wolf (Cajun Lady);

As Themselves: Lee Corso, Bill Cowher, Dan Fouts, Chris Fowler, Jimmy Johnson, Brent Musburger, Dan Patrick, Lynn Swann, and Lawrence Taylor.

Dirty Work (MGM, 1998) 81 minutes, PG-13-rated.

Credits: Producers: Brad Grey and Robert Simonds; Director: Bob Saget; Screenplay: Frank Sebastiano, Norm Macdonald, and Fred Wolf.

Cast: Norm Macdonald (Mitch); Jack Warden (Pops); Artie Lange (Sam); Traylor Howard (Kathy); Don Rickles (Hamilton); Christopher McDonald (Travis Cole); Chevy Chase (Dr. Farthing); Adam Sandler (The Devil—uncredited); Gerry Mendicino (Manetti); A. Frank Ruffo (Aldo); Deborah Hinderstein (Charlotte); Gary Coleman (Himself); Chris Farley (Jerry); John Goodman (The Mayor); Ken Norton (Himself); Matthew Steinberg (Mitch at Age Fourteen).

Big Daddy (Columbia, 1999) 95 minutes, PG-13-rated.

Credits: Producers: Sid Ganis and Jack Giarraputo; Director: Dennis Dugan; Story: Steve Franks; Screenplay: Steve Franks, Tim Herlihy, and Adam Sandler.

Cast: Adam Sandler (Sonny Koufax); Joey Lauren Adams (Layla Maloney); Jon Stewart (Kevin Gerrity); Cole Sprouse/Dylan Sprouse (Julian); Josh Mostel (Mr. Brooks); Leslie Mann (Corinne Maloney); Allen Covert (Phil); Rob Schneider (Delivery Guy/Homeless Guy); Kristy Swanson (Vanessa); Joseph Bologna (Mr. Koufax); Peter Dante (Tommy); Jonathan Loughran (Mike); Steve Buscemi (Homeless Guy); Tim Herlihy (Singing Kangaroo); Jacqueline Titone (Waitress); Kelly Dugan (Kelly); Jared Sandler (Jared); Jillian Sandler (Jillian); Steven Brill (Castellucci); Michael Giarraputo (Hoboken Motorist); Steve Glenn (Guy at Party); Al Cerullo (Helicopter Pilot); Dennis Dugan (Reluctant Trick-or-Treat Giver).

Deuce Bigalow: Male Gigolo (Touchstone, 1999)
PG-13-rated. [In Production]

Credits: Producers: Sid Ganis, Barry Bernardi; Executive Producers: Jack Giarraputo and Adam Sandler; Director: Mike Mitchell; Screenplay: Harris Goldberg and Rob Schneider.

Cast: Rob Schneider, Arija Barreikis, Marlo Thomas; Oded Fehr, William Forsythe, Gail O'Grady, Eddie Griffin, Adam Sandler.

Little Nicky (New Line Cinema, 2000) [In Production]

Credits: Producers: Jack Giarraputo and Robert Simonds; Director: Steven Brill; Screenplay: Tim Herlihy and Adam Sandler.

Cast: Adam Sandler, Harvey Keitel, Patricia Arquette, Rhys Ifans, Allen Covert, Rodney Dangerfield, Peter Dante, Jonathan Loughran.

TELEVISION

Remote Control (MTV, 1987–90) Half-hour game show.

Adam Sandler as Featured Performer, appearing as Stud Boy and Stick Pin Quinn.

First episode aired December 7, 1987; show canceled as of March 2, 1990.

Saturday Night Live (NBC, 1975–Present)
Ninety-minute comedy sketch show.

Adam Sandler as Staff Writer (1990–91); as Featured Performer (1991–93); as Cast Member (1993–95). His recurring characters included: Audience McGee; Brian, host of the Denise Show; Cajunman; Canteen Boy; Fabio (in *Il Cantore* and *La Cantoria*); One of the Gyro Guys; Halloween Costume Expert; Lucy (of The Gap Girls); and Operaman.

Sandler's first appearance on the series was in the episode broadcast December 9, 1990; his last appearance was on May 13, 1995.

discography

SOLO ALBUMS

They're All Gonna Laugh at You
1993, Warner Bros.
Producer: Brooks Arthur, 64 minutes

Tracks: "Assistant Principal's Big Day," "The Buffoon and the Dean of Admissions," "Buddy," "The Longest Pee," "Food Innuendo Guy," "The Beating of a High School Janitor," "Right Field," "The Buffoon and the Valedictorian," "Mr. Spindel's Phone Call," "The Thanksgiving Song," "The Beating of a High School Bus Driver," "Oh Mom . . . ," "Fatty McGee," "At a Medium Pace," "The Beating of a High School Science Teacher," "The Cheerleader," "I'm So Wasted," "Lunchlady Land," "The Beating of a High School Spanish Teacher," "Toll Booth Willie," "Teenage Love on the Phone," "My Little Chicken."

What the Hell Happened to Me?
1996, Warner Bros.
Producers: Brooks Arthur and Adam Sandler, 75 minutes

Tracks: "Joining the Cult," "Respect," "Ode to My Car," "Excited Southerner Orders a Meal," "The Goat," "Chanukah Song," "The Excited Southerner Gets Pulled Over," "The Hypnotist," "Steve Polychronopolous," "The Excited Southerner Gets a Job

Interview," "Do It for Mama," "Crazy Love," "The Excited Southerner Meets Mel Gibson," "The Adventures of the Cow," "Dip Doodle," "The Excited Southerner Proposes to a Woman," "Memory Lane," "Mr. Bake-O," "Sex Or Weight Lifting," "What the Hell Happened to Me."

What's Your Name?
1997, Warner Bros.
Producers: Brooks Arthur, Allen Covert, Jon Rosenberg, and Adam Sandler, 64 minutes

Tracks: "Moyda," "The Lonesome Kicker," "Bad Boyfriend," "Pickin' Daisies," "Corduroy Blues," "Listenin' to the Radio," "Sweet Beatrice," "Dancin' and Pantsin,'" "Zittly Van Zittles," "Four Years Old," "Voodoo," "The Respect Chant," "The Goat Song," "Red Hooded Sweatshirt."

Stan and Judy's Kid
1999, Warner Bros.
Producers: Brooks Arthur and Adam Sandler, 72 minutes

Tracks: "Hot Water Burn Baby," "Cool Guy 1," "7 Foot Man," "Peeper," "Cool Guy 2," "Dee Wee (My Friend the Massive Idiot)," "Whitey," "Cool Guy 3," "She Comes Home to Me," "Champion," "Cool Guy 4," "Chanukah Song Part II," "Inner Voice," "Cool Guy 5," "Welcome My Son," "Psychotic Legend of Uncle Donnie," "Reprise."

COMPILATION ALBUMS

Adam Sandler sings "Grow Old with You" on the 1998 Warner Bros. album, *The Wedding Singer, vol. 2*. On the 1999 Sony soundtrack album to *Big Daddy*, Sandler is heard in dialogue snippets.

on the internet

OFFICIAL WEB SITES

Adam Sandler

www.wbr.com/sandler

This opening page for Warner Bros.' Sandler-related sites features entertaining, informative Web pages on *What the Hell Happened to Me?*, *What's Your Name?*, and *Stanley and Judy's Kid.*

Adamsandler.com

www.adamsandler.com

The most comprehensive Sandler page on the Internet, set up and run by Jack Giarraputo and Allen Covert. Contains information on all of Adam's CDs and movies, as well as behind-the-scenes pictures from his tours and recording sessions. A good place to link to official movie/CD sites as well.

Adam Sandler's Home Page

www.asandler.com

Adam's own home page, with jokes, drinking games, and a picture of a man with his head up his a**. You can send Adam e-mail from this site.

Big Daddy

www.spe.sony.com/movies/bigdaddy/splash.html

Sony's official *Big Daddy* site, with much behind-the-scenes information on the film.

The Waterboy

www.thewaterboy-themovie.com

Touchstone's official site for *The Waterboy*.

The Wedding Singer

www.weddingsinger.com

New Line Cinema's official site for *The Wedding Singer*.

FAN SITES

There are far too many unofficial Adam Sandler–related Web pages to list individually. They range in quality from the outright amateurish to the truly professional. Virtually all of them feature pictures and Sandler quotes. Many also have sound clips, video clips, and other Adam-related materials. Here are a few of the best as well as an Adam Sandler–focused user/newsgroup entry:

Adam Sandler Newsgroup

alt.fan.adam-sandler

A newsgroup devoted to Adam, where fans post messages discussing various aspects of his career/life. Activity here is sporadic, picking up considerably with the release of a new Sandler product (CD, movie, etc.).

The Adam Sandler Shrine

www.geocities.com/Hollywood/Guild/4507

This site—in the words of its own creator—contains "way more than is healthy for anybody to know about Adam Sandler."

Adam Sandler: Star of the Millennium
www.angelfire.com/on2/voodoocity/sandler.html

One of the most exhaustive repositories of Sandler-related material on the net, with a chatroom, fan fiction, pictures, sound clips, and a news page that is updated at least once a week.

Watergirl's Adam Sandler page
www.geocities.com/Hollywood/Trailer/5969

One young lady's shrine to Adam Sandler, with tons of pictures, sound clips, and Sandler sightings as reported by "Watergirl" and other fans. Don't miss the animated goat at the bottom of the page.

NOTE: The Web addresses given previously are subject to (constant) change. A good way to find Adam Sandler fan sites is by visiting a Sandler webring (a group of pages centering around a common interest). You can find those rings by going to www.webring.org and doing a search for Adam Sandler.

SATURDAY NIGHT LIVE

It's Saturday Net
ccwf.cc.utexas.edu/~serpas/snl.html

Frank Serpa's *SNL* episode guide is an invaluable reference tool, giving airdate, host, musical guest, and a fairly complete list of sketches for each *SNL* show.

NBC: Saturday Night Live
www.saturdaynightlive.com
(also accessible via www.nbc.com/snl)

NBC's official Web site features information on the current cast, as well as highlights from previous seasons. Good stuff, but better by far is the following site.

Sean Bradley's Saturday Night Live Page
www.saturday-night-live.com

Features cast biographies, cast lists organized by year, *SNL* trivia, and many valuable links. A good starting point for your *SNL*-related Web explorations.

bibliography

PERSONAL INTERVIEWS

Clemons, Michael. Telephone conversation. June 15, 1999.

Schiavone, Robert. Telephone conversation. June 17, 1999.

Thompson, Bill. Telephone conversation. August 6, 1999.

SOURCES OF OPENING QUOTES OF CHAPTERS

Introduction
King, Susan. "He's Got a Soft Spot in His Heart for the Fonz." *Los Angeles Times,* November 6, 1998.

Chapter 1: The Outsider
Berkman, Meredith. "Adam Sandler is a Very Funny Guy." *Mademoiselle,* March 1995.

Chapter 2: The Class Clown
Telephone conversation with the author.

Chapter 3: The Big City
Weeks, Janet. "For Adam Sandler, Moments Where His Heart Hurts a Little." *USA Today,* February 13, 1998.

Chapter 4: The Big Break
"Saturday Night Live." People, September 25, 1989.

Chapter 5: Great Expectations
Stahl, Sandy. "Adam Sandler Laughs at Reports of *SNL's* Decline."
(Allentown, Pennsylvania) *Morning Call*, October 29, 1994.

Chapter 6: Back to School
America Online Chat Transcript. February 5, 1998.

Chapter 7: Starting Over
"Sandler, His Eye on H'Wood, Leaving N.Y.-Based 'SNL.'" *New York
Daily News*, July 7, 1995.

Chapter 8: Different Strokes
Sherman, Paul. "Comic's *Airheads* Adds Character to 'Adam Family'
Lineup." *Boston Herald*, July 31, 1994.

Chapter 9: Going to the Chapel
Layton, Eric. "The Big '80s." *Entertainment Today*, February 13–19,
1998.

Chapter 10: The Big Breakout
Strauss, Bob. "Sandler Sings a Different Tune (Sort of)." *Los Angeles
Daily News*, February 16, 1998.

Chapter 11: Big Bucks
Schaefer, Steven. "Daddy Big Bucks." *Boston Herald*, June 20, 1999.

Chapter 12: Big Daddy
Layton, Eric. "The Big '80s." *Entertainment Today*, February 13–19,
1998.

Chapter 13: The Last Word
Layton, Eric. "The Big '80s." *Entertainment Today*, February 13–19,
1998.

BOOKS AND PERIODICALS

"Adam Sandler's 'Polychronology' to Debut on Comedy Central." *PR Newswire*, February 12, 1996.

Anderman, Joan. "*Waterboy* Overflows with Repellent Humor." *Boston Globe*, November 6, 1998 (review).

Anderson, John. "*Waterboy* Is Strictly for Sandler Connoisseurs." *Los Angeles Times*, November 6, 1998 (review).

Ansen, David. "A Sweet-and-Sour Sandler." *Newsweek*, July 5, 1999 (review).

Baldwin, Kristen, with Zack Stentz. "Just Kiddin'." *Entertainment Weekly*, May 14, 1999.

Bark, Ed. "Infantile Sandler Pacified by Career Track." *Dallas* (Texas) *Morning News*, February 10, 1995.

Bash, Alan. "Movies Beckon, but for Spade, *SNL* Is Home." *USA Today*, April 3, 1995.

Beale, Lewis. "In *Airheads*, Adam Sandler Plays His Favorite Type of Character: An Idiot." *New York Daily News*, August 3, 1994.

Beck, Henry Cabot. "*Bulletproof* Funnier Than You'd Expect." (New Orleans, Louisiana) *Times-Picayune*, September 13, 1996.

Beck, Marilyn and Stacy Jenel Smith. "Casting Hell." *Los Angeles Daily News*, September 10, 1999.

———. "Grumpy Old Man Jack Lemmon Isn't Grumbling About His Income." *San Diego Union-Tribune*, March 8, 1996.

_____. "Success of Gross-Out Flicks Begets More of the Same. *Los Angeles Daily News*, July 16, 1999.

Belcher, Walt. "Most *SNL* Players Fade into Oblivion." *Tampa* (Florida) *Tribune*, July 10, 1995.

Berkman, Meredith. "Adam Sandler Is a Very Funny Guy." *Mademoiselle*, March 1995.

Bianculli, David. "Adam No Bomb, Just Not Side-Splitting." *New York Daily News*, October 11, 1996 (concert review).

"The Big-Screen Scene," *Los Angeles Daily News*, December 12, 1996.

Brannigan, Kristin A. "The New Batman and Robin of Comedy." (Los Angeles) *Valley Vantage*, September 5, 1996.

Brelis, Matthew. "Teen Tastes Set the Agenda for the Rest of Us." *Denver Post*, April 13, 1999.

Brown, G. "Adam Sandler Can't Resist Urge to Rock." *Denver Post*, July 5, 1996.

Brown, Phil. *Catskills Culture*. Philadelphia, PA: Temple University Press, 1998.

Cader, Michael. *Saturday Night Live: The First Twenty Years*. Boston, MA: Houghton-Mifflin, 1994.

Calk, Samara. "*SNL's* Sandler Makes 'em Laugh." *Capital Times*, March 7, 1994.

Campbell, Laurie. "*Waterboy* Star Dumped—Days Before Wedding." *National Examiner*, December 22, 1998.

Carr, Jay. "Calculated *Big Daddy* Will Please Sandler Fans." *Boston Globe*, June 25, 1999.

_____. "Review of *Billy Madison*." *Boston Globe*, February 13, 1995.

_____. "Sandler the Best Man for *Wedding Singer*." *Boston Globe*, February 13, 1998 (review).

Carter, Bill. "A Comedy Institution Just Keeps on Going." *New York Times*, September 19, 1999.

Carvell, Tim. "Dearly Beloved, Valued Customers, and Members of the Media." *Fortune*, November 24, 1997.

Carver, Benedict and Dan Cox. "Sandler Draws Sony into Toon Tuner." *Daily Variety,* January 20, 1999.

Cetner, Marc and Ellen M. Goodstein. "Wedding Bells for *Wedding Singer* Star." *National Enquirer,* January 23, 1999.

Chetwynd, Josh. "Sandler Moves from *Wedding* to Getting *Kid.*" *Hollywood Reporter,* February 13, 1998.

Christon, Lawrence. "Anarchy in the USA." *Daily Variety,* February 9, 1996.

Christy, George. "The Great Life." *Hollywood Reporter,* June 25–27, 1999.

Citron, Alan. "Saturday Night Fever." *Los Angeles Times,* November 21, 1992.

"Comedy Smarminator Takes His Act to the Big Screen-O-Rama." *New York Times,* November 19, 1993.

Cook, Kevin. "Checking in with Adam Sandler." *Playboy,* February 1999.

Corliss, Richard. "Going Goofy at the Movies." *Time,* June 21, 1999.

_____. "The Next Worst Thing." *Time,* September 16, 1996.

_____. "Sandler Happens." *Time,* November 23, 1998.

Cortina, Betty. "Stop the Presses." *Entertainment Weekly,* June 18, 1999.

Cox, Dan. "For $5M, NL 'Weds' Sandler." *Daily Variety,* February 27, 1996.

_____. "New Line's Latest Is Sather-Apatow Pitch 'Holiday Shopping.'" *Daily Variety,* December 4, 1996.

De Vries, Hillary. "Drew Barrymore's Fractured Fairy Tale." *Los Angeles Times,* July 19, 1998.

Dreher, Rod. "Is Comic Adam Sandler the New Jim Carrey?" *New York Post,* November 10, 1998.

Ebert, Roger. "Review of *Mixed Nuts.*" *Chicago Sun-Times,* December 21, 1994.

_____. "Review of *The Wedding Singer.*" *Chicago Sun-Times,* February 13, 1998.

Everett, Todd. "Review of *Saturday Night Live.*" *Daily Variety,* October 24, 1994.

Ferman, Dave. "Funny, How?" *Fort Worth* (Texas) *Star-Telegram,* July 8, 1996.

Ferraro, Michael X. "Reviews of *The Waterboy.*" (Los Angles) *Entertainment Today,* November 6–12, 1998.

Ferrer, Esteban. "Scribe Duo Scripts Success." *Daily Variety,* March 9, 1999.

Fink, Mitchell. "But Is She Home by Curfew?" *People,* March 11, 1996.

Fleming, Michael. "Chris Farley Leaving *SNL* to Make Films." *Chicago Sun-Times,* July 12, 1995.

Freeman, Miller. "Arthurian Legend." *Studio Sound,* May 1998.

Fuson, Brian. "*Big* Biggest Sandler Pic." *Hollywood Reporter,* June 28, 1999.

Garner, Jack. "Wanted: More Work for Three Neat Guys." *Gannett News Service,* August 4, 1994.

Gaudiosi, John. "Wedding Bells." *University Reporter,* February 1998.

Glieberman, Owen. "Light as a Father." *Entertainment Weekly,* June 25, 1999 (review).

_____. "Review of *Airheads.*" *Entertainment Weekly,* August 19, 1994.

Goldstein, Patrick. "Cut-Rate Comedy." *Los Angeles Times,* May 11, 1997.

Goldworm, Adam. "Hollywood Stoops to Conquer." *Los Angeles Times,* July 11, 1999.

_____. "*SNL*'s 'Opera Man' Hits B.O. High Notes." *Variety,* October 20, 1997

Graham, Nancy Perry. "Insider." *People,* November 23, 1998.

Graser, Marc. "Webheads Open Peepers Wide for Sandler's Short." *Daily Variety,* September 8, 1999.

Graham, Renee. "Rat Pack Returns." *Boston Globe,* November 16, 1997.

Green, Tom. "Sandler on a Hot Streak." *USA Today,* April 8, 1994.

Grove, Martin. "Buddy Action-Comedy Formula is *Bulletproof.*" *Hollywood Reporter,* September 11, 1996.

Hall, Jane. "NBC Looks to Restore the Shine on *SNL.*" *Los Angeles Times,* July 14, 1995.

Hamilton, Kendall and Yahlin Chang. "Oh, You Silly Boy." *Newsweek,* November 9, 1998.

Harrington, Richard. "Review of *Airheads.*" *Washington Post,* August 5, 1994.

Hearne, Christopher. "She Charmed the Boxer Shorts off Him." *Kansas City Star,* June 27, 1996.

Henson, John. "The Dating Game." *US,* February 1999.

Hershenson, Karen. "*Saturday Night Live*'s Adam Sandler Is 'Happy' to Move into Films." *Knight-Ridder/Tribune News Service,* February 15, 1996.

Herz, Steve. "*Wedding Singer* Star Is a Mama's Boy." *National Enquirer,* March 10, 1998.

Hill, Doug. "Can *Saturday Night* Regain Its Bite?" *New York Times,* October 2, 1994.

Hinson, Hal. "Daddy Love." *Los Angeles Times,* June 24, 1999 (review).

Hobson, Louis B. "Adam Sandler's Family Too Big to Meet the Press." *Edmonton* (Alberta, Canada) *Sun,* June 20, 1999.

Holden, Stephen. "Review of *Bulletproof.*" *New York Times,* September 6, 1996.

Honeycutt, Kirk. "Review of *Big Daddy.*" *Hollywood Reporter,* June 18–20, 1999.

Jakes, Edie. "The Director Boy." (New York City) *Resident,* November 20–26, 1998.

Jensen, Jeff. "A Show of Force." *Entertainment Weekly,* March 25, 1999.

Jevens, Darel. "A True Test for Sandler: His Star Role in *Madison.*" *Chicago Sun-Times,* February 12, 1995.

Johnson, Allan. "Sandler Carving Out a Career Even a Mother Could Love." *Chicago Tribune,* February 29, 1996.

Johnson, Dean. "Punch Lines and Bass Lines." *Boston Herald,* June 14, 1996 (concert review).

Justin, Neal. "Dumb Luck." *Minneapolis Star-Tribune,* June 18, 1996.

Kalk, Samara. "*SNL*'s Sandler Makes 'em Laugh." *Capital Times,* March 7, 1994.

Karger, Dave. "The Fall Guy." *Entertainment Weekly,* November 20, 1998.

Kast, Marlise. "Revealed: Why Adam Sandler Can't Find Love." *Globe,* December 22, 1998.

Kempley, Rita. "Review of *Billy Madison.*" *Washington Post,* February 11, 1995.

King, Susan. "He's Got a Soft Spot in His Heart for the Fonz." *Los Angeles Times,* November 6, 1998.

Kit, Zoriana. "Brill to Direct Sandler in NL Darling *Nicky.*" *Hollywood Reporter,* August 12, 1999.

Klady, Leonard. "Review of *Airheads.*" *Daily Variety,* August 1, 1994.

———. "Review of *The Wedding Singer.*" *Daily Variety,* February 12, 1998.

Knight-Ridder News Service. "Adam Sandler Hopes to Leap from Late Night TV to Big Screen." *Asheville* (North Carolina) *Citizen-Times,* February 10, 1995.

Koehler, Robert. "Review of *Big Daddy*." *Daily Variety,* June 18, 1999.

Koltnow, Barry. "Rob Schneider Won't Copy *SNL* Act." *Phoenix* (Arizona) *Gazette,* July 1, 1995.

Koseluk, Chris. "Adam Up!" *Hollywood Reporter,* March 10, 1999.

LaSalle, Mick. "Heavy-Metal *Airheads* Actually Has Substance." *San Francisco Chronicle,* January 13, 1995 (review).

Laski, Beth and Michael Fleming. "Sandler, Wayans Cut *Bulletproof* Deal." *Daily Variety,* July 17, 1995.

Layton, Eric. "The Big '80s." (Los Angeles) *Entertainment Today,* February 13–19, 1998.

_____. "Jon Stewart Gets Serious." (Los Angeles) *Entertainment Today,* June 25–July 1, 1999.

Levy, Arie. "The Chosen." *New York Times,* July 19, 1999.

Leydon, Joe. "The Lawman and the Weasel." *Houston* (Texas) *Press,* September 5, 1996.

Lovell, Glenn. "Review of *The Waterboy*." *Daily Variety,* November 6, 1998.

Mackie, Rob. "What's All the Fuss About Adam Sandler?" (London) *Guardian,* April 16, 1999.

Martin, Ed. "*SNL* Exposed." *Inside Media,* May 27, 1992.

Maslin, Janet. "Mud Dogs! Mud Dogs! Rah Rah Rah!" *New York Times,* November 6, 1998 (review).

_____. "Review of *The Wedding Singer:* Something Borrowed: '85." *New York Times,* February 13, 1998.

_____. "What Happens When a Little Boy Meets a Very Big Baby." *New York Times,* June 25, 1999 (review).

McManus, Kevin. "Review of *Airheads*." *Washington Post,* August 5, 1994.

Mehle, Michael. "One Happy Camper." *Denver* (Colorado) *Rocky Mountain News,* July 8, 1996.

Mendoza, Manuel. "NBC's Struggling *Saturday Night* Has Lost Its Liveliness." *Dallas* (Texas) *Morning News,* March 19, 1994.

Meyers, Kate. "Adam Ribs." *Entertainment Weekly,* February 17, 1995.

_____. "Adam Sandler—Face to Watch." *Entertainment Weekly,* September 17, 1993.

"Michael O'Donoghue Writer for *Saturday Night Live,*" *Associated Press,* November 10, 1994.

Miller, Jay N. "Sandler's Comedy, Rock Stir the Crowd." (Quincy, Massachusetts) *Patriot Ledger,* June 17, 1996 (concert review).

Mink, Eric. "*SNL* in a For-Lorne Position." *New York Daily News,* May 17, 1995.

_____. "*SNL* Will Be Different, but at 19, Can It Be Fresh?" *New York Daily News,* September 25, 1993.

Mukherjee, Tiarra. "Lights FM." *Time,* January 19, 1996.

Nashawaty, Chris. "Green Light District." *Entertainment Weekly,* June 18, 1999.

Natale, Richard. "Sandler Fathers a Hit in *Big Daddy.*" *Los Angeles Times,* June 28, 1999.

_____. "Something About Sandler." *Los Angeles Times,* November 10, 1998.

"New *SNL* VIP," *Minneapolis Star-Tribune,* August 31, 1995.

O'Hehir, Andrew. "Review of *The Waterboy.*" *Sight and Sound,* May 1999.

O'Steen, Kathleen. "U's *Madison* an Avenue for *SNL* Comic Sandler." *Daily Variety,* April 15, 1994.

Pearlman, Cindy. "Awed Adam." *Entertainment Weekly,* July 29, 1994.

People, "Best and Worst Dressed '99," September 20, 1999.

Petrikin, Chris and Benedict Carver. "Sandler, *SNL* Renew Vows." *Daily Variety,* February 23, 1998.

Pfefferman, Naomi. "From Operaman to Leading Man." *The Jewish Journal,* February 13, 1998.

Pickle, Betsy. "Sandler's Dream: Actor Man." *Knoxville* (Tennessee) *News-Sentinel,* August 5, 1994.

"Pop Eye." *Los Angeles Times,* May 16, 1999.

"The Power List: The 100 Most Powerful People in Hollywood," *Premiere,* June 1999.

"Premiere's Ultimate Summer Movie Preview," *Premiere,* June 1999.

Puig, Claudia. "Jeepers! Sandler's 'Peeper' Woos Web Creepers." *USA Today,* August 17, 1999.

"Rapper Up," *People,* March 23, 1998.

Rechstaffen, Michael. "Review of *Billy Madison.*" *Hollywood Reporter,* February 13, 1995.

_____. "Review of *Happy Gilmore.*" *Hollywood Reporter,* February 16–18, 1996.

_____. "Review of *The Waterboy.*" *Hollywood Reporter,* November 6–8, 1998.

_____. "Review of *The Wedding Singer.*" *Hollywood Reporter,* February 12, 1998.

_____. "Sandler-Wayans Duo Misfires in *Bulletproof.*" *Hollywood Reporter,* September 6, 1996 (review).

"Review of *Happy Gilmore.*" *People*, February 26, 1996 .

"Review of *The Wedding Singer,*" *Movie Gazette,* February 13–19, 1998.

Rice, Lynette. "Littlefield Signs *Daddy* Scribe." *Hollywood Reporter,* July 22, 1999.

Rodman, Sarah. "Sandler Schticks to Likable Moron Role." *Boston Herald,* June 17, 1996.

Roman, Monica. "Couple Takes *Wedding* to Heart at ShowEast." *Variety,* October 20–26, 1997.

Rosenthal, Phil. "Live from Aspen, It's a Tribute!" *Los Angeles Times,* March 23, 1997.

_____. "*Saturday Night Live* Far from Dead." *Los Angeles Daily News,* May 14, 1994.

Rozen, Leah. "*Big Daddy.*" *People,* July 5, 1999.

Rubin, Saul. "Daddy Doubles the Joys of Gross Misconduct." *Los Angeles Times,* June 25, 1999.

Rutenberg, Jay. "Rejecting Sandler Lite." *Boston Globe,* March 14, 1998.

Salem, Jon. *Adam Sandler, Not Too Shabby.* New York: Scholastic, 1999.

Salem, Rob. "Lifeless From New York." *Toronto* (Ontario, Canada) *Star,* May 28, 1994.

Sandler, Adam [comedian/actor]. Interviewed by Ben Stiller, *Interview,* December 1994.

Sandler, Adam [trade journalist]. "Adam Sandler." *Daily Variety,* July 16, 1996 (concert review).

_____. "Opera Man Flying Solo." *Daily Variety,* March 9, 1999.

_____. "Sandler Charts Success." *Daily Variety,* January 27, 1994.

"Sandler Backs Off Quote." *New York Daily News,* February 15, 1995.

"Sandler, His Eye on H'Wood, Leaving N.Y.-Based *SNL.*" *New York Daily News,* July 7, 1995.

Sandler, Judy. Interviewed by Adam Sandler, "Funny Boy." *Seventeen,* November 1998.

"Sandler 'Misquoted,'" *Hollywood Reporter,* February 14, 1995.

"Sandler Plans Toon Project." *Associated Press,* June 21, 1999.

"*Saturday Night Live.*" *People,* September 25, 1989.

Schaefer, Steven. "Daddy Big Bucks." *Boston Herald,* June 20, 1999.

Schickel, Richard. "Review of *Billy Madison.*" *Time,* March 6, 1995.

Schneider, Karen S. "Last Laugh." *People,* November 30, 1998.

Schruers, Fred. "Review of *The Waterboy.*" *Rolling Stone*, December 10, 1998.

Schwarzbaum, Lisa. "*Bulletproof.*" *Entertainment Weekly*, September 20, 1996, (review).

Searleman, Eric. "What's Your Name?" (Phoenix) *Arizona Republic*, November 20, 1997.

Sherman, Paul. "Comic's *Airheads* Adds Character to 'Adam Family' Lineup." *Boston Herald*, July 31, 1994.

Shulgasser, Barbara. "Elementary Filmmaking." *San Francisco Herald-Examiner*, February 10, 1995 (review).

Slotek, Jim "Getting the Last Laugh." *Toronto* (Ontario, Canada) *Sun*, October 2, 1994.

_____. "Shooting the Breeze with Billy." *Toronto* (Ontario, Canada) *Sun*, February 11, 1995.

Smith, Christy. "I Dumped Adam Sandler—for Being a Nerd!" *Globe*, July 27, 1999.

Smith, Kyle and Maria Speidel. "Daddy's Boys." *People*, July 19, 1999.

Snierson, Dan. "The Entertainers." *Entertainment Weekly*, December 25, 1998–January 1, 1999.

Snyder, Michael. "Q and A with Kevin Nealon." *San Francisco Chronicle*, July 10, 1994.

Stahl, Sandy. "Adam Sandler Laughs at Reports of *SNL*'s Decline." (Allentown, Pennsylvania) *Morning Call*, October 29, 1994.

_____. "Comic Adam Sandler Is a Big Man on Lafayette Campus." (Allentown, Pennsylvania) *Morning Call*, November 5, 1994.

Stein, Ruthe. "Sandler's Antics Make Him 'Happy.'" *San Francisco Chronicle*, February 11, 1996.

Stimac, Elias. "Christine Taylor Leaves Brady Bunch Image Behind." *Drama-Logue*, February 12–18, 1998.

_____. "Drew Barrymore Joins New Line's Wedding Party." *Drama-Logue*, February 12–18, 1998.

_____. "*SNL* Alumni Adam Sandler Gets New Gig as Wedding Singer." *Drama-Logue,* February 12–18 ,1998.

Strauss, Bob. "Nothing Sacred in *Wedding.*" *Los Angeles Daily News,* February 13, 1998.

_____. "Sandler Sings a Different Tune (Sort of)." *Los Angeles Daily News,* February 16, 1998.

Sullivan, Jim. "Who Are You Calling Stupid?" *Boston Globe,* November 17, 1998.

"Success of Gross-Out Flicks Begets More of Same," *Los Angeles Times,* July 16, 1999.

"10 Fun Facts You Didn't Know About Adam Sandler," *Globe,* November 24, 1998.

Theimer, Sharon. "Fellow Comedians Weep for Chris Farley." *Associated Press,* December 23, 1997.

Tianen, Dave. "Sandler's Act Needs to Take a Mulligan." *Milwaukee Journal-Sentinel,* June 19, 1996 (concert review).

Travers, Peter. "Valentine from A Crazy Man." *Rolling Stone,* March 5, 1978, p. 73.

Turan, Kenneth. "A Snapshot of Coming Attractions." *Los Angeles Times,* March 28, 1999.

"The 25 Most Intriguing People of the Year," *People,* December 28, 1998–January 4, 1999.

Vigoda, Arlene. "Iron-Man Bob Barker." *USA Today,* February 13, 1996.

Vincent, Mal. "Sandler Breaks Through in Odd Film." (Norfolk) *Virginian-Pilot,* August 6, 1994.

Walker, Dave. "New Cast Members Seek to Bring Life Back to *Saturday Night.*"(Phoenix) *Arizona Republic,* September 23, 1994.

Wallace, Amy. "Accounting for Taste." *Los Angeles Times,* December 21, 1998.

_____. "An *SNL* Update." *Los Angeles Times*, February 23, 1998.

"Wayans More Than Stand-up Comedian." *Orange County* (California) *Register*, September 6, 1996.

Weeks, Janet. "For Adam Sandler, Moments Where His Heart Hurts a Little." *USA Today*, February 13, 1998.

Weiner, Jennifer. "Critics Scorn Adam Sandler's Dopey Humor, But it's a Hit with Audiences." *Knight-Ridder/Tribune News Service*, February 22, 1996.

Weingrad, Jeff. "*Saturday Night Live* at 25!" *TV Guide*, September 25–October 1, 1999.

Weinraub, Bernard. "A Goofball Guy's Guy." *New York Times*, November 13, 1998.

_____. "What Makes Boys Laugh?" *New York Times*, July 23, 1998.

West, Nancy. "Former NH Class Clown on *Cosby Show* Tonight." *The* (Manchester, New Hampshire) *Union Leader*, December 3, 1987.

Whipp, Glenn. "Sandler's *Waterboy* Awash in Laughter." *Los Angeles Daily News*, November 6, 1998 (review).

Willman, Chris. "Adam Sandler Proves Even the Losers Get Lucky Sometimes." *Chicago Tribune*, December 30, 1994.

Winget, Kelly. "Manchester Youths Get Chance to Show Their Talent." *Boston Globe*, May 2, 1999.

Wloszczyna, Susan. "Sandler Derails on the *Daddy* Track." *USA Today*, June 24, 1999 (review).

INTERNET AND ONLINE SOURCES

Barrymore, Drew. *People Online,* February 1998.

Bruno, Mary (editor). "Adam Sandler Hits the Road." *Mr. Showbiz,* June 13, 1996.

_____. "Backstage at the MTV Movie Awards." *Mr. Showbiz,* June 11, 1996.

Gotz, Stu. "Adam Sandler in the Concert Hall!" *Entertainment Ave!* June 29, 1996, (concert review).

"NBC Bullies New *SNL* Castmembers." *TV Guide Online.* August 17, 1999.

Sandler, Adam. America Online Chat, February 1998.

_____. *E! Online,* November 1998.

_____. *People Online,* February 1998.

Silverman, Stephen M. "Sandler's Fame Game." *People Online Daily,* March 9, 1999.

Szymanski, Michael. "Berg on Slater, Sandler, and 'Bad Things.'" *Mr. Showbiz,* November 27, 1998.

Wells, Jeffrey. "Brooks vs. Sandler." *Mr. Showbiz,* June 10, 1999.

www.eonline.com

www.hollywood.com

www.imdb.com

www.mrshowbiz.com

www.nyu.edu

www.spec.sony.com/movies/bigdaddy

www.wbr.com/sandler

index

about the author

DAVE STERN IS ALSO THE AUTHOR (with Kevin McKeown) of *Your Secrets Are My Business* (Longstreet, 1999), as well as the best-selling *The Blair Witch Project: A Dossier* (Onyx, 1999).

The author, who has also been employed as a record producer, book editor, and telephone solicitor, now lives in Northampton, Massachusetts, with his wife, daughter, and the world's two pointiest dogs.

For more information visit *idt.net/~dastern* on the Internet.

Also available from Renaissance Books

The Girl's Got Bite: An Unofficial Guide to Buffy's World
by Kathleen Tracy
ISBN: 1-58063-035-9 • $14.95

Movie Stars Do the Dumbest Things
by Margaret Moser, Michael Bertin, and Bill Crawford
ISBN: 1-58063-107-X • $14.95

That Lawyer Girl: The Unauthorized Guide to Ally's World
by A. C. Beck
ISBN: 1-58063-044-8 • $14.95

Don't Call Me Marky Mark: The Unauthorized
Biography of Mark Wahlberg
by Frank Sanello
ISBN: 1-58063-071-5 • $16.95

Matt Damon: The Unauthorized Biography
by Chris Nickson
ISBN: 1-58063-072-3 • $16.95

The Ultimate Bogart
by Ernest W. Cunningham
ISBN: 1-58063-093-6 • $16.95

The Ultimate Barbra
by Ernest W. Cunningham
ISBN: 1-58063-041-3 • $16.95

To order please call 1-800-452-5589